Waldenbook store
new Orleans
april 1976

A Classical Education

ROBERT WOODS KENNEDY

A Classical Education

W · W · NORTON & COMPANY · INC·

NEW YORK

Copyright © 1973 by W. W. Norton & Company, Inc.
FIRST EDITION

Library of Congress Cataloging in Publication Data
Kennedy, Robert Woods.
A classical education.
I. Title.
PZ4.K358Cl [PS3561.E4272]   813'.5'4   73-9752
ISBN 0-393-08370-5

1 2 3 4 5 6 7 8 9 0

A garden inclosed is my sister, my spouse;
a spring shut up, a fountain sealed.

Song of Solomon, 4:12

Part One

I

When I was fourteen, my mother and father were divorced. My mother and I moved to Paris. She put me in a boarding school there. It was only four blocks from her apartment, but felt continents away. It was a gloomy time for me.

I walked a lot, exploring Paris. Eventually I discovered a beautiful garden and square. There was a great fountain in the garden, with statues of a large, naked, muscled, bearded man and two smaller, naked, smooth voluptuous women surrounded by sheets of noisy water. They were black with soot. I thought of them as the three P's, the Palpably Phallic Paragons. Around the pool in front of them was a gravel terrace, shady, with chairs for hire. I read there. The garden made me want to be a landscape architect. A beautiful gilt and wrought iron gate near the fountain led to the rue du Bouc, a short street, which led to the square.

The square was deeply arcaded on three sides. The fourth was a neoclassic stone theater, with steps all along its front, an Ionic colonnade, and five ornate entrances. On its axis, in the middle of the square, was a circular island with a tree and a low stone monument called "The Coffin" in the neighborhood, then an Avenue leading to a Roman temple in the far distance, Corinthian, actually a church. The rue du Bouc, and its continuation on the other side of the square, the rue des Chèvres, made a cross axis. A grand scheme. It made me want to be an architect.

Under the high and commodious arcade, to the right of the rue du Bouc, was a residential hotel favored by writers and newspapermen of all nationalities. On the left, an artists' supply store, smelling of oil, turpentine, gum and pigments kept in bulk. Next some doors to basements and to the apartments above. Next a coffee store which filled that corner of the square with the smell of roasting beans and chicory. Then more doorways, the corner one magnificent, diagonal. Facing the theater, the shoemaker, hugely mustachioed, who worked in his window and wanted another war with *les sales Boches,* more doors, the pastry shop, smelling divinely, and the Post Office, where one phoned, and which purveyed a variety of bureaucratic discomforts.

Symmetrical with the Post Office, across the Avenue, was the Police Station. Very young cops in blue capes strolled in and out, or bicycled slowly there and away. They were being trained for duty in more elegant or more dangerous neighborhoods. Then the cabinetmaker, always in a rage of craftsmanship, doors, the wine shop where I bought cider to remind me of our farm, doors, and a corner entrance symmetrical with the other. Then the tobacconist, most of his perfumed or acrid wares in bulk. I occasionally bought a single cigarette there to smoke on the street. It was romantic, like eyeglasses, and made me feel delightfully woozy.

Then the English Book Store, on the corner of the rue des Chèvres, a low deep place, jammed with books, smelling of books, existing for books, publishers of contemporary writing. It also sold and lent them, but I felt those to be secondary functions. There was a desk at the back where a plump, voluptuous Greek girl, Micini, typed manuscripts and took one's money. I read many novels there, perched on a pile of them, in a corner. I could have borrowed them, and did sometimes, but I felt welcome, and enjoyed the cross-examinations on my reading exacted as tribute by Micini and the proprietress. I guessed they had money troubles. The atmosphere was of quiet, frantic dedication. Many writers dropped in. I loved the place.

Next, the rue des Chèvres, the only medieval street in the quarter. It went off from the square at a slight angle to one's left, was short, dark, too narrow for sidewalks, and sloped uphill. Midway on the left was the milk goats' stable, half underground. A very low door, usually open, let them in and out. It was stygian inside, despite a tiny bulb which burned day and night. I liked the raw goat smell. It, too, reminded me of our farm. Directly opposite was a magnificent Gothic entrance with steps leading up to a bricked-up door, a favorite spot for artists by day, lovers by night. It was known as "The Standup" in the neighborhood and was woven into numberless ribald remarks.

The side door to the *bistro* was on the rue des Chèvres, the front was on the square, directly opposite the hotel. Its terrace occupied three arches of the arcade, and was marked off by a boxwood hedge, growing in a row of wooden boxes. Its front was complicated, all glass with many mullions, many curtains opened and closed at random. Inside, a long, dented zinc bar, behind it the *Patronne* by day, the *Patron* by night, the waiter, it seemed, always. Paralleling the windows was a row of round white marble tables, with four chairs at each, which squeaked, agonizingly, when moved. The clientele varied according to the hour. The one more or less sure customer was the taxi driver, whose stand was in front. He became a special friend of mine. It was a not-too-clean, well-lighted place at night, a clean dim cave in the daytime, the scene of a million tipsy conversations, ribald, puzzled, irate, tearful, searching. It smelled of new coffee, hot milk, old wine, old beer, and old disinfectant.

Next to its front door, on the end wall of the arcade, was a stenciled sign: DÉFENSE DE PISSER. I translated it into English and into German, which I was taking in school, as my fancy pleased. The *pissoires* of Paris were papered, inside, with frightening posters describing and illustrating the effects of syphilis. The local brothel, No. 5, was not on my beat.

The neighborhood was peaceful. There were few young children, very few youthful men. They were in the army, or had left. There were many formidable widows and many self-absorbed young women. Almost everybody wore felt slippers, some, heavy round-toed leather boots, some, pointed patent leather boots. The men wore shirts with long tails, which formed their underpants. The collars and cuffs were detachable. Most of them had mustaches, a sign they had been in the war. Nearly every *concierge* had a dog, fat white pigs rather than proper canines. Everyone, of every age, shook hands, a quick pump, when arriving and when leaving. It was a mania.

There was an air of controlled bustle about the place.

2

When I was sixteen I moved into the hotel. It had a beautiful glass entrance. Inside five steps led up to a small marble lobby. On the right, the *concierge*. On the left, towards the front, the office of the Notary Public. At the rear, the stairs, six stories up to my room, one story down to the kitchen and cook's quarters. She was a special friend, and my confidante.

The stairs wound around a small well. On the first, third, and fifth landings were two water closet compartments, on the second and fourth, bathtub compartments. Someone was usually going up or down a half flight to one or the other. They smelled of disinfectant. The tub compartments had monstrous, dangerous water heaters in them. One ordered a bath from one's waiter in advance, who drew and announced it. They were charged for separately, and required a separate tip.

My door was at the top of the stairs. To its left a table and chair for my waiter, a kindly, crotchety old ostrich and my self-appointed mentor, then the speaking tube to the kitchen, then the dumb waiter. The door itself was narrow and low. The room was large and splendid. As one entered, the front wall was to the right, the back wall to the left. The long wall opposite sloped in. It was the underside of the mansard roof. On the back wall a lavatory, with one spring-handled cold water faucet, under it a portable tin *bidet*, flowers painted all over it, on a rattan stand. Next, a huge *armoire*. In the corner my phonograph and records, jazz and classical. My mother did not like Brahms. "He's a tunesmith. Second-rate Beethoven." I had a lot of his music, as a gesture of independence, and particularly liked the tunes of the Third Symphony. But my true love was Dvorak's New World Symphony. I played it every day, sometimes twice, and could whistle the whole thing. American jazz appealed because of its soul weariness, French and British because of their simplistic gaiety. I danced by myself, to the jazz records, imagining a warm girl in my arms. At the farm I had danced with my dog.

Opposite the door was a large sideboard with a large plan of the Piazza San Marco over it, a filigreed silver alcohol stove on its top, and a kettle to heat water for tea and shaving. Inside was a vast assortment of tools and supplies, including a small collection of postcards: the "Aphrodite of Cyrene," my favorite; Courbet's *"Le Sommeil"*; Titian's "Venus of Urbino"; Giorgione's *"Concert Champêtre"*; Barbari's "Mars and Venus," another favorite; a bevy of beautiful, romantic, nude women, but none of them quite right for me. Courbet's brunette was too big in her bottom, Barbari's Venus's thighs and right arm were too long, Cyrene had no head. Buying the postcards was a problem, particularly at the Luxembourg where the lady at the concession, a terror, would say, "All you boys buy that," and laugh.

Next to the sideboard, my drafting table, perpendicular to the wall, very large and low, with the stool beyond it, back to the front wall. In the corner, piles of books on the floor.

The front wall had a great double casement window, looking out on the square, in a recess with a comfortable window seat under it, a large low coffee table in front. Then a table and three chairs, then a low bed alcove with a small double casement giving a charming, raking view of the theater's colonnade. The bed was huge, high, laden with pillows and puffs, a terror to make in its narrow confines. The window sill, as wide as the window seat, served as a bed table. The alcove could be closed off by a heavy curtain. "To keep out the night air," my waiter said. I never used it. On the floor, at the foot of the bed, was my fur rug. The floor itself was magnificent—black walnut herringbone. It glowed. There were two pipes along the sideboard wall near the floor, for heat. It was turned on and off according to an ordained schedule, which had nothing to do with the weather. The pipes cracked, banged, groaned, and hammered as they filled with steam, then hissed. Between the bed alcove and the door was a Chinese scroll I had saved up for and bought. It was of the leaves of a tree silhouetted on a paper screen.

The middle of the room was empty.

Part Two

3

One late summer day, in 1927, when I was seventeen, I got a *pneumatique* from my mother asking me to dinner that night. I was delighted. I liked my mother a lot, and knew that the food, drink, and conversation would be of the best. My allowance was late. I had no money and would have had to eat in my hotel, or borrow from my waiter. Neither prospect appealed. It did not occur to me to acknowledge my mother's invitation. I read *War and Peace* and played the New World Symphony until an hour before the appointed time, ran down the five flights, and started off to walk the four enchanting miles of Parisian streets and *quais* between my hotel and my mother's apartment.

I loved my mother's apartment, the street it was on, and the building it was in. I took the gilded birdcage lift up through the center of the stairwell, got off, and rang. Her man Friday opened the door, beamed, then expressed, in pantomime, his disappointment at not being able to relieve me of a hat, coat, gloves, scarf, or stick. I patted him, went to the kitchen door, and stuck my head in to say good day to his wife. They were both superb cooks, both ingenious gougers. My mother enjoyed these attributes to the full, reveling in their cooking, while detailing, in her charming and fluent English, their latest larcenous scheme. Friday opened the *salon* door and announced me.

My mother, supremely beautiful, was in a characteristic pose, reclining, indolently, on a sofa opposite a small fire, wearing a charming bare-shouldered white Empire evening dress, her hair in a *chignon*. Her face, however, was invisible to me, as it often was. Next to her was Victor, her tawny Pomeranian, looking alert and interested. He wagged his tail furiously for a moment. At right angles to the sofa, on rather than in an armchair, was the most beautiful live girl I had ever seen. I judged her to be seventeen too. Her name sounded French. Her first name was Sarah. I immediately forgot her last. She did not offer her hand, or say anything. She simply smiled at me, enchantingly.

When I had come in, my mother was, as usual, talking like mad. After introducing us she immediately resumed her theme, which was the Paris theater of the last season. I was too stunned to pay much attention. My first impression of Sarah was of someone normally big, but as I took her in I realized that she was quite small. When she was finally able to say a few words, I realized that she was an American. She sat on the edge of her chair, hands in her lap, breasts thrust forward, back straight, somewhat in the contrived position of Victorian young ladies, but with a difference. She was not contriving, she was expressing, unconsciously, a tremendous eagerness, curiosity, receptivity. She was literally and emotionally on the edge of her seat, as people say of audiences at an exciting performance. She was absorbing, with all her might, every aspect of my mother, her clothes, furniture, apartment, servants, conversation—everything, I thought, except me. She was meltingly cool to me.

Her beauty put me in turmoil. I could not look at her face very often. It was too luscious. I felt I had to learn it in small steps. My mother switched the conversation to the New York theater. Sarah knew an astonishing amount about it—had been, it seemed, to every play for years. She knew many actors and actresses, some also known to my mother. They gossiped. I concentrated on acting at ease. It was not too hard. My mother was a born hostess, entertaining, vivacious, in an incomparably French style. She swept us along, giving me the familiar feeling of being propelled by a rushing brook of sounds. We laughed, were amazed, seemed to reach heights of perception we did not realize we were capable of.

I gradually formed a more concise impression of Sarah. I guessed that she must come from a rich theatrical family. She was stunningly dressed. I knew, from experience with my mother, how much that could cost. She had long, straight black hair, parted in the middle, swept back tightly over tiny pierced ears with barbaric Russian bronze earrings, to a bun low on the back of her neck. A large fan of a necklace and two bracelets which matched the earrings. Sad black eyes, small black eyebrows, very dark eyelids. A perfect nose. An incredibly tempting very full mouth which seemed, in itself, to be love. A round full face. No makeup. My impression was of depth, both psychological and physical, but I had been conditioned to think of girls as fragile, and so felt confused about her. She was dressed like a society girl, such as my mother usually collected, but was plainly not. She did not seem to be a social climber, though she played up to my mother. Everybody did that. Above all I felt that she was highly creative, and became sure that my mother, who adored and collected talented people, thought so too. I could not place her.

After dinner, as delicious as expected, with an hilarious account of Friday's latest larceny, I began to fall in love. I didn't just sit there and fall in love. I worked at it, sensing a bottomless, dangerous, mysterious emotional vortex, and welcoming it. I knew that my mother would become aware of this, she knew me too well and was too perceptive not to, and that she would watch me with glee, laughing up her—strictly speaking—nonexistent sleeve. I didn't care. I just hoped that she would not, this once, crack wise.

Much later I realized that we were staying on and on. It was very late. I was prepared to stay all night. Finally my mother stood, saying to me, "Love, why don't you take Sarah home."

I said, inwardly, "Bless you, Mother dear."

In the foyer Sarah had nothing to get. No purse. I surmised that, like my mother, she must put bills in the top of her stockings, and hoped that unlike my mother she would not make a production of getting them out. I disliked that routine, but liked Sarah's freedom of things. I thought about pockets for girls as we waited for the lift, and while my mother indulged in her usual endless and highly complimentary goodbyes. As we got into the gilded birdcage I knew absolutely that my mother, as she turned away, would say to herself, "That'll fix him!"

Because of her delays, the lights went out halfway down. In the dark I thanked my mother, silently, specifically, for handing over to me this marvelous, mysterious nymph.

Out loud I said, softly, slowly, "Our mother, which art in the fourth floor, Hallowed be thy name, Thy kingdom come, Thy will be done, In Earth as it is in the fourth floor, Give us this day no more daily bread, we're stuffed, And forgive us our inadequacies, As we don't forgive those who inadequate against us, And lead us into temptation, BUT . . ."

Sarah laughed. I've fooled you, I thought. The cage clanged to a halt. I struggled with the gates and, unpremeditatedly, put my arm around her, to guide her down the three familiar steps to the front door. It came as a surprise that she was not ethereal and did not object. I called for the *cordon*, opened the huge wrought iron and plate glass door, with its marvelous bronze hardware, invisible in the dark but wonderful in the hand, and we stepped down onto the sidewalk. Her waist was firm, sinuous, and finally overpowering. Suddenly, horribly, I collapsed into one of my Dithering Idiot moods, and said, "I'm sorry that I can't take you home because I don't have any money but I will get you a taxi and put you into it."

"Don't be silly," she said, as an order, put her right arm through my left, and started to walk. My mother did that "to leave your sword arm free." There was no jockeying about. I realized that she was highly coordinated, even athletic. My Dithering Idiot mood disappeared in, tentatively, a joyful discovery. Beautiful, stylish young girls, it seemed, might also be human. But I was by no means absolutely sure of that.

We walked silently, rapidly, physically pent-up after our long sedentary evening, then gradually slowed down to a saunter. I asked her where she lived, to discover that she was in a hotel very much like my own, diagonally opposite mine in the same block, facing the garden, and that she went to the square and to the rue des Chèvres every day. She said, "I don't know anything about what it's really like, just what it looks like. Tell me."

I suddenly felt very talkative, and gave her a complete description of my hotel, my waiter, the life in the neighborhood, The Standup, the shopkeepers, the taxi driver, the cops, the *Patronne* of the *bistro,* its clientele, and what the square was like on nights when the theater was alive. She listened with dreamy absorption. After a while she gradually turned towards me, as we strolled along, until her breast was pressing against my arm. I savored that warm pressure as I had never savored anything before. I assumed it was unconscious and hoped she would not discover she was doing it, and stop. When she looked up at me I felt hot flashes of emotion. When she looked down I thought I was boring her. When she looked away, I felt rejected. Between crises, I savored with her the lovely empty early morning Paris streets and *quais,* and their details as they swam in and out of the gas lights, cobblestones, manhole covers, curbstones, parapets, balustrades, and undersides of leaves, the soffit of a colonnade, steps leading down into blackness. We got to her hotel door after three. She leaned, stunningly stylish, against its stone jamb. In great fear that she would say "No," I asked if I could see her the next day.

"Yes. At four o'clock," she said and vanished, in a sophisticated way.

I walked to my room mad at myself for having talked so much that I had learned nothing about her, threw my clothes on the floor, and lay sleepless until dawn, reviewing the evening.

"Head over heels in love," I said to myself.

4

I woke up when my waiter knocked and opened the door, around noon. He said, "You were out very late last night. Night air is bad for the health."

The thought of Sarah surged through my body. I sat up. He had become invisible, but continued, "It's bad for clothes to be left on the floor. They don't last if one treats them like that."

He was bustling about, so I assumed that he was picking them up and putting them in the *armoire*.

"Don't you want some lunch?"

Another overpowering wave of Sarah engulfed me.

"Are you all right?" he asked, suddenly solicitous.

"Yes. No. I don't know."

"Ah, you're in love then."

"That's for sure."

"Well, it happens to everybody at one time or another. Come, let me get you something to eat. It will help."

"O.K."

"You shouldn't use that."

He left, mercifully. His reference was to my American father, who lived in New York, and of whom he did not approve, "in principle." He adored my mother. Without principle?

I fell into a state of being which I had known since early childhood as "waiting" in which it was impossible to do anything except anticipate a longed-for event.

When he brought lunch I asked if I had a letter.

"Of course not. If you had, I would have put it on your tray."

There was a long pause, during which I blanked out everything.

"Do you need money?"

"Yes."

"People in love always need money."

"People without money need money."

"You must understand that people in love need more money than those who are not in love."

"Why?"

"But it's obvious!"

There was another long pause, during which I was finally able to see him.

"I will lend you the appropriate amount."

"Thank you very much," I said, wondering how much it would be.

At three my longing for Sarah became unbearable. I went downstairs, picked up the money at the *concierge,* which, uncannily, was exactly the amount I would have asked for if he had given me the chance, and walked around the corner to her hotel. It took three minutes, so I walked around and around our block at top speed, seeing it with new eyes. Each time around I crossed the street to the garden side at her hotel and paused, to memorize its façade. At three-thirty I walked into the lobby knowing that as I could not remember her last name, the *concierge* was going to give me a hard time. I was not disappointed. Finally she decided to give in, and said, "Oh, you mean Mademoiselle Sarah on the first. Why didn't you say so to begin with? It would have saved all this time and trouble."

She tapped a code on a bell, Sarah's waiter appeared, a more merciful edition of my own, obviously intrigued, ushered me up the stairs to her door, knocked, opened it, and said, "There is a handsome young man here to see you, Mademoiselle."

"Thank you."

She smiled at me, silently, expectantly. I simply couldn't say anything. She ordered tea in a French Canadian accent, standing sideways to the door, immobile, enormously alive. Her nipples showed, her legs were bare. She had a sketchbook and an eraser in one hand, a pencil in the other. I asked, "May I see your sketchbook?"

She had just started that sketch so it told me little. I flipped back through the pages, more and more impressed as sketch followed sketch. She *was* talented, as I had surmised the night before. The book was a graphic diary. There were drawings of her hotel, the street, scenes in the garden, chic women with emphasis on clothes, a beautiful nude pulling a dress over her head, The Standup, and dress designs. I asked, "Have you been to art school?"

"No. I just picked it up."

"How long have you been in Paris?"

"Three weeks."

"How long will you be here?"

"I don't know."

"Why are you here?"

"To see Paris. It's something I've always longed for."

"When you leave where are you going?"

"To London."

"Why? It's awful there. Foggy."

"I'm going to go to school there, to study stage design."

"Why not in New York?"

"It didn't seem a good idea."

"Why not here? It's lovely here."

"I hadn't thought of it."

"Do you design your own clothes?"

"Yes."

"And make them?"

"Yes."

"What does your father do?"

"He's dead."

Damn, I thought, why don't I abide by my mother's advice and not ask direct questions. I came across a beautiful drawing of an extraordinarily pretty woman with her arms around her head, in bed, asleep.

"Who is that?"

"My sister."

"What's her name?"

"Josephine."

"Tell me about her."

"She's eight years older than I am. She lives here. That's one of the reasons I came. She's married to a French perfume manufacturer, and they have two little girls. I'm not very fond of her, but she's nice enough. And I am, originally, French Canadian. Now that's enough."

"Excuse me. I'm sorry. I can't seem to help it. I want so much to know all about you. Do you mind?"

"Yes."

She seemed to fall into a serene, silent trance.

And that, I thought, is that—for the moment.

Her room was more elegant than mine, a rectangle. The front wall had two sets of French doors, with heavy curtains, opening on tiny wrought iron balconies overlooking the garden, an elegant Louis XVI desk, chair and mirror between them. One short wall held the *armoire* and the lavatory, with a curtain beneath, hiding, I was sure, the inevitable portable *bidet*. The other held a loveseat, two comfortable chairs, and a low round inlaid wood table, a small lacy brass rim around the edge of its top, as if it was meant for a ship. The inner wall held the usual big high bed, laden with puffs, pillows and spreads, easy to make, with a chest of drawers on each side. There was an elaborate cornice, an elaborate circular plaster decoration in the middle of the ceiling, and a decorated plaster dado. While my room could be anywhere, hers was indubitably French. Mine is as good a place to work in, I thought, as this is to play social games in. I hoped she didn't play them.

Her waiter brought tea. We sat down in the comfortable chairs, Sarah silhouetted against the French doors, with the sun sparkling in the leaves of the trees in the garden behind her. She was too beautiful. I could think of nothing to say. She asked, "Would you like cream, or sugar, or both?"

"No, thanks. Just tea."

"How is it that you live in a hotel all by yourself?"

"Because I got fed up with boarding school, and threatened to go on strike if I couldn't live by myself. My school has both boarding students and day students. I became a day student."

"But your mother told me you were an architect."

"I've been in architectural school for half a year. I was half a year ahead, all I had left to do was the final examinations. So I went to architectural school."

"And how is it, living alone I mean?"

"Lonely."

"How come your parents let you?"

"My father takes no interest. He doesn't have custody. I suppose he might write me a despairing letter if I got poor marks. But I don't, so he doesn't write. I don't write him, except when my allowance is late."

'And what about your mother?"

"I think she saw the problem as an equation in inconveniences. I don't mean she doesn't love me. She does. But if I had just stopped and failed, or got kicked out, it would have been a blow to her. Kids who fail impinge on their parents' comfort. If I had run away it would have been a disaster. If she had insisted I live with her, she would have had a sullen brat on her hands twenty-four hours a day, with the possibility I might be miserable enough to do miserably in school—a tremendous inconvenience. So she bowed to my solution, graciously, and we found my hotel. I moved in with a tremendous sense of relief and gratitude, which I still feel, when I think about it."

"So now you will simply go to architectural school. Would you like some more tea?"

"Yes. I really want to be an architect, and have for a long time. But at the moment I'm mixed up about it because of the *Patron* of my *Atelier*. We call him Old Stroph, because his favorite word is '*catastrophe*.' Everything is a '*catastrophe*.' He is, at bottom, a kindly man. Also he's a marvelous draftsman. But he puts us off so we won't bother him. He's a tyrannical sub-deity, pompous, overpowering, insistent on a norm. There's only one way to do anything, according to him. The *Beaux-Arts* formula. It's completely silly. So he's brutal in his criticisms, really completely unfeeling for the student's individual bent. We're not supposed to be individuals. We're supposed to be reflections of him, and of the arcane mysteries of the school's tradition, which isn't very old anyway, and doesn't fit today's needs and possibilities.

"Another thing that upsets me about Old Stroph is that he doesn't know anything about construction. Construction, according to him, is beautifully drawn, shaped and arranged blocks of India ink, *poché* it's called, presumably indicating brick or stone, never concrete or steel. The patterning of *poché* is an art in itself. The abstract design is what's important, not what's really happening."

"Are there alternatives?"

"Many. But the architects I find most interesting don't teach, at least formally. Have you heard of Le Corbusier and Pierre Jeanneret, or André Lurcat, or Eileen Gray and Jean Badovici, or of the rue Mallet-Stevens?"

"No. What is the rue Mallet-Stevens?"

"A street of cubist houses, named after their architect. I'd love to show it to you. Let's go."

I got up. She picked up her sketchbook, pencil, and eraser, and we left. I wondered, again, about where she kept her money, but decided not to ask, to wait and see.

It was too late to walk both ways to the rue Mallet-Stevens. We went to the *bistro* in the square to get the taxi driver. He wasn't there so we sat down in the arcade to wait. I asked, "Would you like an *apéritif?*"

"No, thanks. I don't drink."

"On principle? You had some wine last night."

"No. It's simply that I can't. It does something to me. But one glass of wine is all right. I'll have a *Vichy* to keep you company."

I ordered, feeling overcome with delight at being able to get her something, lovely Sarah, in that beautiful arcade, behind that beautiful boxwood hedge.

"Have you heard of Professor Piatagorsky?" I asked her.

"No. I know far too little about architecture, which is one of the reasons I'm going to go to school. It's a large part of stage design, in a sort of secondary, abstracted way. Tell me about him."

"He's the best, I think, of the Parisian architects, the most interesting, the most up-to-date. He has a large office, but it's mostly architectural engineering for other architects. His own output is small. His son Pytor is one of my best friends, and also goes to Old Stroph. I think of going to study with him, but he teaches at the École Polytechnique, and changing involves a host of difficulties, political, bureaucratic, personal, and academic, like degrees."

The taxi driver came back. I introduced him to Sarah and we got in.

"Where to?" he asked.

"Rue Mallet-Stevens."

"You have a mania for that place. You'll end up living there."

"Never," I said, shocked at myself, as I realized that while that was the direction I wanted to take, I wanted to live in a classical environment. Bramante was still my favorite architect. Am I already tainted, I wondered, and determined to talk to Pytor about it, when next we met.

"You'll stay in the Square then?"

"Yes."

"Has Mademoiselle been there?"

"No."

"She won't like it, you can be sure."

"Why not?"

"It's not feminine."

"It's not supposed to be. It's supposed to be architecture, cubist, mechanistic, modern."

"It doesn't look much like Mademoiselle."

"But why, good God, should it?"

"It would be a lot more attractive if it did."

I slammed shut the glass screen, cross with him. When we were there, Sarah got out, fascinated, and walked along the sidewalk. He said, "Do you want me to wait?"

"No. We'll walk back."

"But it will take you all night."

"I hope so."

"Ah, it's like that, is it? Then I think you're saved. Just a few curves in the right places would help this street extraordinarily."

"You're an art critic."

"But naturally."

I had never thought of architecture as having a feminine aspect, or of the taxi driver as a connoisseur of women.

After Mallet-Stevens we walked for three hours, Sarah occasionally making sketches, while I watched her adoringly, had dinner, and walked for three more hours, the last one in an intense exchange of our impressions, intuitions, savorings, discoveries of the aesthetics of the route we were taking, I wanting a much more intimate exchange, fascinated, frustrated. When we got to her hotel I asked, "May I come to see you tomorrow, earlier?"

"No. I'll come to see you, at four o'clock," and, as she had the night before, she managed to disappear in a most mysterious and rapid fashion.

I realized, as I walked back to my hotel, that we had been together for nine hours, that I had again talked too much, that she had led me on, and that she had been really noncommunicative about the facts of her life, while extraordinarily communicative about her perceptions.

Is she, I asked myself, really terribly shy?—hiding something?—afraid of men? How long will I have to wait? Is she really a different breed, after all? If so, what am I going to do for the rest of my life? Will gentleness help? I pondered these questions until dawn.

5

The next three days we started off a little earlier each day and added more modern architecture, churches, tombs, boat rides, and dance halls to our walks, meals, and Sarah's sketches. She danced divinely. I asked her if she had had lessons.

"Well, yes, but not formally. I never went to dancing school. It's just more exhilarating than going to a gymnasium."

Her beauty disturbed me constantly. I felt I would have to come to terms with it by many separate acts of will. When we entered a restaurant, or walked by groups of workmen, it was an occasion, for them and for her. The thread of our exchange would be broken and would have to be started again. Because of my mother, I was more or less familiar with this problem. But whereas it wryly amused me in her case, it pained me in Sarah's. I was willing to share my mother. I did not want to share Sarah. Her marvelous clothes, bare legs, and jutting nipples compounded my discomfiture.

She probed me about my life. I was very ready to talk about some of it. In my lonely days in the hotel I had reviewed those parts of it having to do with the farm, consciously and thoroughly. But I had not reviewed, and found it difficult to talk about, boarding school life, which I loathed, and my father, whom I hated.

The farm was near Boston, in New England. I had resurrected: my dog, St. Christoph, an irresistible French Briard, a bundle of grey fur when dry, a skinny rat when wet, full of wiles and love; my boat, the most precious object I owned, its beauty, the excitement it afforded, the release of long lonely sails, during which the rest of the world ceased to exist; a favorite uncle, drunk on prohibition Orange Blossoms, painstakingly teaching me chess on the squares of our living room rug, with a cane but no pieces; canoeing alone, up to the source of the river, among the hot aromatic pines and the snapping turtles to the point where I was in a little nest of overhanging bushes, lost to the world; a horrible scene in which the farmhands had driven a great woodchuck into the river and were trying to drown him; my favorite farmhand, George, his predictions of my future based on the bubbles on the top of his black early morning coffee, in the kitchen, of his warm, sly jokes (no bubbles, no future), of his saving me from certain wrath when I had stolen a recalcitrant horse, and a carriage, to take a pretty cousin for a drive in the woods; Ma, our cat, her offerings of mouse skins neatly laid out on the kitchen porch each morning, her numerous accouchements in front of the kitchen fireplace, her run-ins with catbirds; devastating trips to my grandmother's where I fell off chairs, spilled ice cream, and got shiny new dimes I didn't know what to do with; my beautiful Aunt Helen's supremely beautiful Swedish lover, naked, deeply tanned all over; lying on the rock in our swimming pool, a quiet peaceful enlargement of the river, overhung by trees, a natural dam at its downstream end; my kissing Aunt Helen, avidly, sexually, and of my distress and her complete calm; my six Rhode Island Red hens, one of whom I wanted in bed with me at night, and of my mother's coming in and throwing her out the window; an approach from a homosexual soldier in the town movie house, and of my puzzlement about him; "I love you's" and other weird invitations from my girl cousins and their friends, which I rejected as crazy or scary; my feelings about clipper ships, boats and ships in general, of all times, and their beauty; a young cousin, fully developed and enormously pretty, feeling her breasts, unconsciously, standing in the living room doorway, as she was being sent off to bed; seagulls, fishing for clams, and dropping them on stones near the beach, to swoop down and extract the clam within the broken shell; the feeling of long, sloping, seemingly endless rows of vegetables in the hot midsummer sun, and of the disastrous effects of eating as many small hot cucumbers as I could hold, for a moment; the fascination of ant colonies discovered under large flat stones in the hay fields; the discovery of architecture as a dramatic form of expression in our old, unused mill, in the din of water roaring over the dam; of the orchards, of apples, peaches, pears, apricots, in orderly rows; above them on the southern slope, the vineyard, a tangled maze of vines, stakes, and strings. A halcyon time if one left out the bad parts. I made sketches for Sarah of houses, dogs, trees, boats, ships, to illustrate, and maps to elucidate.

She forestalled my asking the same of her. She seemed to dislike direct questions, but then, most people did. Nor did she respond to indirect probing if it might lead to information rather than opinion or intuition. I did discover that she had worked for a repertory theater. And I began to feel that, given her intelligence and intensity, she was undereducated. She had not read as much, or heard as much music as, somehow, I would have expected, and she seemed to know no history. She was enigmatic. I got more and more curious, more and more desirous of her, and more and more frustrated. She seemed unapproachable at times, warm and outgoing at others. I felt she did not love me as I loved her, because if she had, she would want to share memories of her life with me, as I wanted to share mine with her. Above all I felt weak in relation to her, dared not kiss her, or buy her flowers, or hold her hand, or say "I love you."

Late in the afternoon of our fifth day together we had tea in my room, on my window seat, facing each other, our cups on the window sill. There was a pause in our talk. I looked at her right hand, relaxed over her thigh, the tips of her fingers spatular, a marvelous tool in repose. I wanted to bend over and kiss it. She said, "I will have been here a month day after tomorrow. I have to get an identity card. And while I'm at it I might as well get a foreign student's card too."

"Are you going to stay, then? You're not going to London? Do stay."

"I don't know. I can't decide. Will you help me get the cards?"

"Yes, if you will have dinner with me here, afterwards."

"What a lovely bargain—for me."

She smiled at me, enchantingly, and went on, "Can we go to see 'Potemkin'? It's supposed to be marvelous."

"Yes," I said, wanting desperately to take her in my arms. "Will you wait here a minute? I want to go see my cook."

"Yes. I love looking at the Square. It's somehow more interesting than the garden, I suppose because there are more people."

I ran downstairs to the kitchen, one of my favorite rooms, small, very high, its windows at sidewalk level on the rue du Bouc, a huge chopping block in the middle, a great black range, always occupied by double boilers, a great copper hood over it, pots, pans, knives, and spoons hanging on the walls, steamy, aromatic, redolent of two hundred years of marvelous meals, the cook ensconced, strong, ribald, intelligent. I told her, "I want to have a friend for dinner tomorrow night."

"Good God! You're getting social. Who is it? It's the beautiful American girl I've been hearing so much about. You're the talk of the neighborhood, you know. At last he's got a girl! at last! I was worried about you, afraid you might be a fairy underneath. Or a religious maniac. Does she eat well?"

"Yes."

"Does she know anything about food?"

"No."

"Few Americans do. You'll have to teach her. Is she young enough?"

"Seventeen."

"That's a bad year, as you very well ought to know. She should be sixteen. That's a nice year. Do you suppose you could persuade her to roll back? Where is she from in America?"

"New York."

"Everybody in America is from New York. Who lives in the rest of the country? It must be absolutely vacant. What do you want to eat? No, don't tell me. Sweetbreads, oyster plant, and potato puffs, true? I'll think of the rest. I know she's upstairs. Hurry back. Don't walk, run. Arrive panting."

6

We met at two the next day and walked fast, under the arcade, to the Police Station. I knew what to expect. Sarah did not. There followed an afternoon of filling out forms, walking blocks to get them stamped, endless waiting, being pointedly ignored, paying tiny fees, and being given contradictory instructions, a typical bout with French bureaucracy. Sarah's beauty was of no help, which made me as cross as its success in other areas. We went back to my hotel frustrated and exhausted, the papers still incomplete, rambled up the five flights and collapsed on the bed, to recapitulate the absurdities, incredulously on her part. After a while we began to see them as funny, and for the first time laughed really intimately together. It made me realize that while Sarah often smiled, she seldom laughed.

We had dinner on the window sill, looking out over the square, enchanting in the soft Paris twilight. The *bistro* was brilliantly lit, the taxi in silhouette against its glow. As dusk grew, lights started to come on, in small blocks, at random, all over the façade of the theater. In half a minute it was transformed from a dour, black, neoclassic Minotaur, in spite of its Ionic order, to a sparkling lady of pleasure. Can it be, I wondered, that the Classic and Romantic modes, which I thought of as polarized, are really only the shove of a knife switch apart? I asked Sarah, "Do you love light bulbs?"

She gave me an amused look.

"They're so romantic. It's incredible. I feel as if we had witnessed the transfiguration of a soul."

"And of a tree. There's a little man in there, in a deep, dark room, with a great bank of knife switches in front of him. He would like to close them in order, but he can't tell which switch does which lights. He wants to see them come on himself some day. But how can he? He's very frustrated."

The gas lighter came along, touching each post with his magic pole. Employees hurried up the steps of the theater. The audience began drifting in, leisurely, anticipatory, at first, then hurriedly. She said, "This must be what it's like to be a gargoyle. Isn't it lovely?"

But her mood, gay at the beginning, steadily darkened. Her eyelids, always dark, got darker. She fell silent, alarming me. I got two candles, put them on the coffee table, lit them, gathered up the dishes, and put the tray out in the hall. This was no moment for an interview with my waiter. When I shut the door I did not lock it, as I had intended, afraid that she might feel trapped. She asked, "Would you like me to dance for you?"

I didn't. I wanted desperately to kiss her. But I said, "I'd love it," and got on the bed to watch. She put on *Swan Lake* at a certain precise point, which told me that this was planned, had been rehearsed. The mood of her dance was ominous, like that of the music. She did it with tremendous intensity. I felt that she was warning me about some aspect of herself which she did not wish to put into words. It touched me. Finished, she took off the record and lay down on the bed beside me. I puzzled about its meaning, not

43

wanting to ask her for an explanation. After a while, out of nothing, not really knowing what I meant, I said, "The Cinderella syndrome?"

"Yes, but more so."

I raised my head to kiss her on the mouth. She turned hers just enough to thwart me. I felt rejected and puzzled, in need of time to think. As we walked to the movie I decided that I would leave her early that night and think about what I could do to break her reserve and my timidity. Or was it, I wondered, that she simply did not like me enough to either confide or kiss.

"Potemkin" is short. We were out sooner than expected, overcome by it, went to the *bistro* to talk, to recall those scenes in which streams of people descend the walkways and steps of Odessa. After a while we fell silent. I thought that I should take her home, but couldn't bear to, in an agony of longing for her. Abruptly, she got up, took my arm and aimed directly for my hotel. In my room we lay down on my bed. After a while she put an arm under my neck and kissed me tenderly. I felt unable to respond, was awkward, felt frenetic. My pendulum had swung too far in the opposite direction. I said, "It's not that I don't love you. I adore you. I love you passionately. It's that I'm too shy, too unsure of myself, too perplexed. I'm too new in the world of you. I'm afraid of hurting you, of pushing you, of frightening you. I cherish you so much I sometimes feel like dying. Please believe me."

"I do," she said, softly, darkly.

I put my arms around her and concentrated on her emanations, signals, signs. She was sad, afraid. I gloomed for a time and, exhausted, fell asleep.

44

7

I woke up, Sarah still beside me, when my waiter knocked and walked in. He looked shocked when he saw us.

"Good Lord, here you are, asleep, with your clothes on, no blanket over you, and the windows wide open. It's bad for one's health. Furthermore, it's very bad for clothes."

"We fell asleep."

"Well, obviously. That's no excuse." He paused. "What would you like for breakfast?"

I told him. Sarah said, "Let's go for a quick walk in the garden before breakfast comes."

We ran down the stairs, going to the W. C.'s on the way, linked arms, and walked fast to the great gilt and wrought iron gate. Sarah's mood was gay and sparkling. The garden shone somnolently in the low morning sun. Just inside the gate, on the gravel walk, with its borders of flowers, she slowed and tilted her head to be kissed. I pecked at her, fraternally.

"No, that's not it," she said, and with her breast against my arm, pushed me to the chairs around the fountain of the three P's. I paid the chair lady. We sat down and faced each other. She brought her face very close to mine, held it there for a long moment, then put her arms around my neck, tilted her head and, infinitely slowly, put her open mouth on mine. I was awkward with her, decided not to try too hard, to practice. She kissed me divinely, while I practiced. Suddenly it started to go smoothly. I put my arms around her and gave her a tremendous hug. We laughed and got down to serious kissing. A long time later I heard the chair lady say, "They're still at it. Isn't that something!"

We got up and went back to my hotel. My waiter was on the landing waiting for us.

"Your breakfasts are ruined."

"I'm so sorry. Forgive me."

"Where have you been?"

"Walking."

"But why didn't you think of your breakfasts?"

"We fell to kissing."

"What!" he said, incredulously. "On empty stomachs?"

"Yes. So now be very kind and get us two new ones."

As he turned to the speaking tube he said just audibly, disgustedly, "Lovers! Eccentrics!"

Breakfast finished, we fell together on the bed, kissed ecstatically until noon, then set off for lunch and the Police Station again. It was the last thing I wanted to do at the moment, but I didn't know what I did want to do, either. I was on an enchanting Paris street, on a dreamlike day, with incomparably beautiful Sarah hanging on my arm. I said, "Damn!"

"Quiet."

It was the first intimate thing she had said to me. Lovely "Quiet." I disengaged my arm and put it around her waist. She gave me the most intimate look I had ever had leveled at me. The concept *femininity* flooded me, wonderfully, wondrously. I gloried in it. She turned and pressed her breast against my side.

The forms completed, we went back to my hotel. As we kissed I began to long to hold her breast but could not bring myself to do it. The thought disturbed me deeply. But the longing became so acute that I finally, automatically, did it, terrified that she would withdraw, as she had when I first tried to kiss her. The sensation was overwhelming.

"Is it all right?" I asked.

"Yes," she said very softly.

With new confidence, I wanted to hold her bare. I undid one of the buttons on her blouse and then, unsure, stopped kissing her and looked a question. She looked a yes. I undid two more buttons, enough to get my hand in, and held her, overcome by a mixture of fear, thrill, and gratitude. After a while I fondled it, very gently.

"Am I hurting you?"

"No," very softly.

I took my hand out.

"Are you all right?" she asked.

"Yes, but it's just too wonderful. I'm so grateful to you. Are you sure you don't mind?"

She kissed me. I put my hand back in. After a while she undid all the buttons. I fondled both of her breasts, too overcome to see them.

We went out to dinner. I realized, on the way down stairs, that I could not remember her breasts, had no clear picture of what they were like. It disheartened me. Dinner was half torture. A longing to hold her again kept sweeping me. When we got back to my room, she stood in the middle, her back to me, took off her blouse, walked to the window seat, sat down and held out her arms. Her breasts were unlike anything in my postcards. I knelt in front of her.

"Kiss me."

After a while we got on the bed. I kissed her from the top of her skirt to the top of her head, knowing that I would remember her breasts forever. I got an erection, my first with a live woman, painfully held down by my shorts. I was appalled at this, and moved away so she would not notice. I came. After a while she said abruptly, "Let's go for a walk," jumped up, put on her shirtwaist, grabbed my hand, and pulled me out the door. On the way back, as we passed her hotel, she said, "I think I had better stay here tonight. Come and have breakfast with me in the morning."

I walked to my hotel, flooded with love and desire. On the first landing I turned around, went back to her room, knocked and entered.

"You're early for breakfast," she said. I took off her shirtwaist with a new found sense of power. We got on the bed and kissed. I held her breasts, got another erection, and came in my underpants. I began to consider putting my hand on her pubis. Finally I did. My penis shriveled. I took my hand away. She found it, put it there, pressing it gently, and kissed me. I pressed her but did not move, entirely overcome.

She had a slit skirt held by an integral belt with a single large button. She undid that, spread her skirt, and put my hand on her vulva, spreading her legs a little. She was fat and round and very smooth skinned there, her slit just perceptible to my palm. I thrilled, tremendously grateful. Holding her was warm, intimate bliss. I came again. She fell asleep. I covered her and lay down beside her in my clothes, to endlessly relive the experience.

8

I woke to Sarah kissing me. She had on a Victorian peignoir. I felt funny in my clothes.

"My waiter will be here soon."

"I love you."

"I'm sorry I fell asleep. But it does show something—that we're peaceful together."

She opened her dress.

"Hold me."

As I put my hand out she spread her legs a little.

"It's so new, so marvelous, but sort of terrifying."

"It's just me. No one else. It's as much a part of me as my nose."

"But your nose terrified me at first."

"I know." She kissed me. "I must pee."

I peed in the lavatory while she was gone. When she got back I said, "Model it for me."

She did, enthralling me. Her waiter knocked, she stopped and called, "Come in."

"Good morning. It's another lovely day," he said.

I realized for the first time that indeed it was.

"Mademoiselle is looking even more radiant than usual."

She smiled dazzlingly at him. I felt a pang of jealousy. My first.

"Mademoiselle's young friend must agree with her."

"But yes," again smiling dazzlingly. She ordered breakfast. As her waiter was leaving it occurred to me that we should get a paper, for the theater news. I asked him, "Is it possible to have a newspaper with breakfast?"

"Good God. You're French."

"No. Half French."

"But that's impossible. You can't be half of something. It's either one or the other."

"Nevertheless, it's true."

"Miracles never cease," he said with emotion. "How does it feel?"

"Confusing."

"I should think so. We don't have papers in the hotel, but I will lend you mine. Just put it on the tray when you're through."

"Thank you so much."

"It's a pleasure," he said and left. Sarah said, "He's right, you know."

"It's a problem."

"Will you be able to solve it? To be either a Frenchman who speaks English, or an American who speaks French."

"I hope so, sooner or later. But I think it's simply a matter of being very much one's self wherever you are. I can't believe that I will ever have to make a conscious choice."

"I have a similar problem, but I want to solve it sooner than later."

"Because your family came from Canada?"

"No, I feel truly American. After all I was born in New York, and have always lived there. I haven't been around, as you have."

"What, then?"

She got up, walked to the far balcony doors, pushed back the curtains, opened them, came back and sat down.

"I'll tell you sometime, but not now. All right?"

"All right."

I thought of her dance.

Our breakfast dishes cleared away, I went to the far doors and stood in them, looking at the garden, thinking about how that particular view looked from other angles, of Sarah's refusal to emerge, of my inability to behave as a man would, forcefully, overpoweringly, of the danger of getting her pregnant, of how to get a condom, of her femininity, and of my determination to cherish as well as to love her.

"Stop thinking," she said. "I can feel you."

"I can't help it. Things are so complicated."

"They're not, really. They just seem so."

She came to me with an undulating walk, which made her peignoir swish, pressed her back against me and put my two hands on her breasts. I held her tight, kissing her ear.

"Kiss me all over."

We went to the bed. I took off her peignoir and kissed her from her stomach, so feminine, so round and swelling, up, but I couldn't look at her thighs or vulva. I soon came. She put her hand on my penis. It collapsed. When it was stiff again she took it, still inside my clothes, and held it firmly. It stayed stiff. It felt marvelous.

"Do you mind?" I asked her. "Is it all right?"

"Yes," she said softly, "I love holding you."

"I'm so glad. You're wonderful."

But it was scary too. I hoped I wouldn't come, scare or shock her. We kissed and fondled until lunch time. I felt tired, emptied, and ravenously hungry. She put on a dress and high-heeled shoes. We set off with two sketchbooks, towards the river, to eat at some sidewalk café on the quai, found a delightful place, and ate grandly, talking about books. She had not read *War and Peace*. When our feast had settled we went for a long walk. On our way back I said, "I'm overcome by your femininity. I love it so. I love your stomach, so round, and your hands, so competent. And you're so generous with it. You make yourself a gift beyond compare. I adore you."

She looked intensely receptive and loving, but made no reply. I wanted one, terribly.

Our path back to her hotel led us by mine. There I said, "Wait. I'll go get you *War and Peace*."

"Meet me in my room. I want to go to the Post Office and call my sister."

We parted. I met my waiter on the stairs. He said, "I understand that you went to Mademoiselle's last night."

"Yes. How did you know?"

"Her waiter told me. He's an acquaintance of mine."

I'm surrounded by spies, I thought.

"He's very reliable."

"I'm very glad to hear that. I cherish Mademoiselle, and want no harm to come to her."

"Rest assured. Is her room nice?"

"Yes, very nice."

"Is it well furnished?"

"Sumptuously. It's also very comfortable."

"Ah, that's good. I'm very glad to hear it. Personally, I've never been in that hotel."

"If her waiter is an acquaintance of yours, why didn't you tell him I'm only half French?"

"I didn't think it would be discreet. Let him find out for himself, I told myself." Pause. "Was it good?"

"Yes."

"The first time is always the best. After that it becomes routine."

I turned and ran up the stairs. In my room I sat down in the window seat to think about it. I realized that Sarah's beauty, her chic, the disparity in our sizes, the intimate way we walked together, her American look, made us very visible in the neighborhood, invited speculation, and that it was inconceivable to our waiters that we could spend a night in her room together without copulating. Well—why hadn't we? I puzzled about it. After quite a while I got the book, went back to her hotel with it. She asked, "What kept you?"

I told her. She said, "Well, about the neighborhood, I can see that. It's not bad. It's just something one has to get used to, even enjoy—because it gives them pleasure, it's something interesting for them, a form of giving for us.

"About our waiters, they love us, want to protect us from the more mundane discomforts. In order to do that for people it's perhaps necessary to spy—sometimes. Don't you feel that about your mother—sometimes?"

"Yes," I said. "She's definitely part of the network."

"And about the copulating," she said, "it's easier said than done."

"Yes," I said gloomily.

"I think we both feel that way."

"I know."

"I love being in your atmosphere. Your room is like you. It has character. Your waiter is like you in that he's a martinet, unlike you in that he is not a puritan. My room is like me. It's a beautiful, unfilled container. My waiter is like me in that he is perceptive, unlike me in that he is transparently himself. It's an odd coincidence, isn't it?"

I felt I had had enough for the moment, got up, handed her the book, and went out onto the balcony. Some Americans came down the street, the girls in ridiculous pastel, multicolored evening gowns, their boyfriends clean apples, crew cut. I called to Sarah. We started to laugh. She said, "Well, that's something neither of us has to face, if for different reasons, and let us thank our stars for it."

I was perched on the side railing of the balcony. She leaned over to kiss me. I put my hands on her bottom, thrilled. After a while she wiggled. I squeezed her nates. After a long while I noticed people in the garden watching us, and froze. She said, "Let's go dancing."

We went to a large student dance hall near by. It was not very full. We danced tremendously intimately. I began to notice that we were the center of attention. It embarrassed me. I froze again.

"Don't stop," she said, "I love it so. Remember what I told you about the neighborhood."

I tried ignoring everybody else, found I could—relaxed. After a while I got an overpoweringly hard erection, painfully held down by my shorts. I knew she must feel it. I stopped.

"I'm sorry," I said.

"Don't apologize. I love it. It tells me that you really want me."

"Are you sure?"

"Yes. Come on. Let's dance."

"It hurts."

"It's bound up in your shorts?"

"Yes."

"Well, in that case, let's go, and let you calm down."

"I'm sorry," I said again.

"Silly, it's great to be that way—we can dance any time we want."

We went to her hotel. She went to the middle of the room and held out her arms. I asked, "What record do you want?"

"I don't mean that," she said.

I undressed her, slowly, voluptuously. When she was naked she asked, "Would you like me to show you four of my good points?"

I sighed. She turned her back to me. I had never really seen it, was overcome. It seemed infinitely complex. She put her arms behind her and pointed with both hands, "Sacral dimples."

They were deep and lovely. I knelt and kissed them. She pointed again, "Lozenge of Michaelis."

I kissed it. She turned around and pointed to the juncture of vulva and thighs.

"No light. Most girls have a space there that you can see through."

She spread her legs. There were two little cups at the top of her thighs corresponding to the bulge of her smooth, plump vulva with its inviting thin furrow.

"Kiss me."

I did.

"Now it's my turn. I want to see your good points."

I froze.

"Yes," she said firmly, and started to undress me. Naked, I leaned on the edge of the bed. We stared at each other. Only her eyes moved.

"You're beautiful."

"No."

"You *are* beautiful. Very. You just don't know it."

"No, I don't."

"I don't suppose boys in boarding schools tell each other that sort of thing."

"No, they don't."

"It's a pity."

"Why?"

"Because if they did, you would already know what a beautiful body you have, that you could be proud of it without vanity, and that it can give others, such as me, extreme pleasure. I want to make a sketch of you, right now."

"Please!"

"It won't take long."

She got her sketchbook and drew. I felt like life class at school, only the other way around. My distress gradually dwindled. When she was through I went over and looked at it. It was very good, and I saw that I was, if not beautiful, at least upstanding looking. It was a surprise. I had never looked coldly at my body.

We got on the bed, kissed. I felt her with more confidence. She felt me. Our nudity was a strange new joy. I got an erection. She said, "Put it in me now."

"What about babies?"

"It's all right," very softly.

I got over her and tried to guide my penis in. She didn't help. I felt awkward, couldn't find the place, and subsided, in misery. She was tremendously loving. Again my penis rose, not very hard, but I found the place, put it in, and immediately subsided. Tears welled out of my eyes, uncontrollably. She kissed them and licked up my tears.

"You're in one of your 'Dithering Idiot' moods, aren't you?"

"Yes. I can't help it."

"They're nice, you know. One of the nicest things about you."

"They're stupid."

"Then be bright. Think about love, not sex."

I did. Surprisingly quickly my penis rose, very hard. I got over her with certainty and put it in. She gently stroked my hand as I did. She moved a little, and then I did. After a while she pulled me down lovingly. We kissed as never before. She made a little sound. I knew that something good had happened, but not what, and in a flood of joy and gratitude, came. I had always supposed that at this moment one felt blissfully content. Instead, I felt ravenous for her.

After a couple of hours we came to a pause. Tears of joy, gratitude, and frustration began to flow. I didn't want them, got up and stood in one of the French doors. Sarah followed.

"Lovely salt tears," she said.

"You're lovely," meaning I'm grateful.

"That's not me," meaning her true self.

"I want you."

"You have me."

"I don't," I said, despairingly.

"No. You don't."

"Join with me."

"If you knew me, would you love me? Truly love me?"

"Twine with me." She did.

"If I could love you, would I?"

"Fuse with me."

"If I knew you, would I love you? Truly love you?"

"Be one with me."

We clung to each other in the cool doorway, not content, aware of footsteps and taxi horns in the street below.

9

I woke up ravenous for her. She was still asleep. I feared to wake her, but after a time could not resist my desire.

"What a lovely way to be wakened," she said, filling me with joy. "I feel like a peach tree in bloom."

We had breakfast and lunch in her room, made love all day, then went out to dinner. On the way back our course took us down the rue des Chèvres and past my hotel.

"Shall we go up, for a change of scene?" I asked.

"No, please. I want one more night in my room."

There, I took off her clothes and mine without the sense of joy I had experienced before. I felt depressed, and wondered why. It swept over me that I had known for some time, and had been suppressing the knowledge from my conscious thoughts, that Sarah had led me skillfully since the day of "Potemkin" but had never said she loved me or offered any endearments. Therefore, she was experienced in this sort of thing and in love with somebody else. I had been taught, not loved. I lay down on the bed. She stood over me, "All right, I'll tell you."

She got on top of me on her knees, sat on my penis. A deep blush started on her neck and spread upward to her forehead, downwards to her waist, and out the tops of her upper arms. Her breasts, arms and face puffed, making her features seem to shrink. Her arms came up and waved, as if she were a marionette. I felt frightened for her and for myself. She said, "You're going to be shocked. Prepare yourself. Don't interrupt me. When I'm through don't ask me any questions. I won't be able to stand it.

"My father and mother were both French-Canadian immigrants to New York. Neither had any education to speak of. My father was a messenger at the New York Stock Exchange. He used most of his small salary to speculate in worthless stocks. It was a mania. We were terribly poor and lived in a slum. When we got hungry my mother would get a job as a seamstress.

"My sister Josephine became a whore when she was fifteen. She's very pretty. She got ahead and catered to rich businessmen. That's how she met Phillippe, her husband. He was in New York on a business trip. He asked her to marry him. She was growing tired of the life, and older. He was rich.

"I've been stage struck ever since I can remember. There was a vaudeville theater in the neighborhood. It was managed by an old man, an acquaintance of ours. He asked me if I wanted to help him clean the house after school, for money. I went, thrilled. I was thirteen, almost fourteen then. He took me down to the coal cellar, beat me, and raped me. When I got home I told my mother I had fallen into a coal scuttle.

"When I was fourteen I decided I was never going to go to school again. I wanted to work in the theater no matter what. I went to the Amsterdam Repertory Theater and asked for a job, lying about my age. I looked old enough to be sixteen. They turned me down, naturally. I hung around there all day every day. I became a sort of mascot. They came to accept me. I slept with any of the older men who asked me. They gave me money or food and explained their jobs. I slept with three or four women too. There are lots of lesbians in the theater."

As she talked she continued waving her arms in that strange way, unconnected with what she was saying.

"They began to give me things to do, errands, all sorts of things. I got more and more useful. Finally they gave me a small salary, sort of under the counter. I got steadily more useful to them. A fixture. That went on for about two years. Then Gordon MacNeill came to the theater."

I knew of him. He was a well known actor, in late middle age.

"I became his mistress. He got me a small apartment on East Fifty-Third Street. I got pregnant. He paid for a gruesome abortion. That's why I can't have babies. He took me around. I learned a lot from him. Then he and his wife got divorced, because of me, and for a number of reasons. Then they got together again, just together, not remarried. He didn't want me around any more. He helped get me a better job with Lawrence Palladine, a really good designer, as general assistant. It included relieving him sexually. He got very busy so he had to give me more and more responsibility. He told me he thought I had talent, but that without any education I'd never get very far. I thought it over. I went to Gordon and asked if he would lend me the money on a long-term basis. He said he would. He advised me to leave New York, in any case, and suggested London. He appointed a mutual friend of ours, Margaret Crichton, as trustee and gave her three thousand dollars in a lump sum to invest and dole out to me as I needed it.

"I've always longed to see Paris, and wanted to see my sister again, so I came here, I thought, on my way to London.

"Miss Crichton is a friend of your mother's. She wrote her giving her, I'm sure, the whole story, or most of it. When I got here I didn't want to see anybody for a while. I wanted to think about my life. Your mother wrote me an invitation. I made an excuse. Then she wrote me again and I felt I had to accept. I went to see her one morning, and of course loved her. She asked me to dinner that night, saying that she would ask you. She told me a little about you. When we met I assumed that she had told you all about me. It made me very sad. Then I realized that she had not. I wanted you, terribly, terribly. I decided not to tell you about me until I had to. So you see I cheated you. I've dreaded this moment more than you can ever imagine.

"One more thing. You may think that I've been acting a part. I haven't. I've never known a person my own age, let alone someone like you. You're just as new and scary to me as I am to you. That's all."

Her flush and swelling gradually subsided, making her eyes and mouth seem to grow. She put her hands on the bed on either side of my head, lowered hers, and stared at me myopically, tragically, hopelessly. I raised my head and kissed her nose. She slowly lowered herself on me, straightened her arms along my sides, exhausted. I thought frenetically for a while and then, too, began to feel exhausted. She began to feel heavy on me. I put my arms around her, rolled her off, put my head on her shoulder, and fell asleep.

10

I woke up knowing that I could not possibly live without her, and uneasy. When I opened my eyes she was directly in my line of sight, sitting on the floor, in front of the doors, back to me, her straight black hair down to her waist, hands apparently in her lap, head bowed. She seemed to be meditating. When I stirred she turned her head, looked at me, then slowly got up and walked halfway to the bed. She was completely made up, eye shadow, mascara, rouge, powder, lipstick, her Venus mound tinted. She had on the barbaric bronze necklace I had first seen her in. I was thunderstruck. I didn't know that she owned any makeup. She said, standing immobile, "I couldn't sleep. I felt so worthless, like such a cheat, so cheap. I looked awful. I didn't want you to see me like that, even for the last time."

I held out my arms to her, beseeching. She walked slowly to me, sat sideways on the bed, and kissed me with infinite tenderness. She was perfumed. After a while she said, "I love you more than I knew."

I felt, incontrovertibly, that she did, that this was the moment I had so often longed for. I had expected it to bring great joy. Instead it brought a heavy sense of responsibility for this beautiful, complex, determined, intelligent, underprivileged live human being in my arms. I felt heavy. She suddenly felt heavy. She said, "Now I don't have to go to London," and fell asleep.

I watched her dream, wondering what awful fabrics

were being generated behind her beautiful moving eyelids. When she woke up I said, "Let's have a bath together."

"Let's. I need one. Will you ask my waiter?"

I found him and asked him to draw us a bath.

"For both of you?"

"Yes."

"Together?"

"Yes."

"I'm sorry, but it's against the policy of the hotel. I am not permitted discretion, you understand. I am really very sorry about this. But my hands are tied." He flung them wide. "What can I do? Please explain the matter to Mademoiselle Sarah."

"I will."

I told Sarah about it and said, "Let's try my hotel."

We found my waiter in the kitchen, talking to the cook. I introduced Sarah to her. She said, "Mademoiselle is even more ravishinug than I had been led to understand."

Sarah gave her a dazzling smile. I asked my waiter, "Would you be good enough to draw us a bath?"

"One for both of you?"

"Yes."

"Together?"

The cook said, "How else could two people take one bath?"

He said, "It's impossible."

"Why?" I asked.

"Because of the public."

"Do you object to two people having a bath together?"

"Of course not."

"Then why does the public?"

"They're different, you should understand."

The cook said, "What he means is that they don't take any baths at *all*. *That*'s why they're different."

Defeated, we went out into the square, sat down on The Coffin, under the tree. There was an incised inscription on the top, proclaiming that a tree would always be grown there in honor of French arboriculture. I could feel the words through the seat of my pants. On the sides were numerous names. It was held in the neighborhood that only English virgins ever read them. There were dappling shadows all over the blackness and whiteness and roundness of Sarah. I kissed her nose. She started a sketch of my right eye, saying, ruminatively, "Sponge baths are nice. Let's go get two large beautiful pans, and four large beautiful sponges from the sea, and have sponge baths together, next to our wash bowls.

"Your eyes are beautiful. So blue.

"I want you to wash me very carefully, from the top of my head to the soles of my feet. Will you be sure not to leave anything out? I want to be cleansed by you, in love and water.

"The shadows dapple and the sun spots dapple because the leaves move, while the sun travels its great arc. In this light you seem to be constantly changing.

"I will bathe you, too, in love and water. Then we will dry each other, tenderly, and then make love, in love, and be informed of each other.

"I have never been loved, only desired.

"I can feel the writing through my skirt, but I can't tell what letters I'm sitting on.

"I know you can and will protect me. And I know I can

let myself be protected by you. You will find that out.

"I hate going to the W. C.'s to pee. You can pee in the wash bowl.

"Move your head a little to your right. Yes.

"I want to get two chamber pots. I can keep them under our beds.

"I think they should be beautiful and identical. Then I won't get pee proud in your room, not that I would anyway. But it will be comforting that way.

"I love the sounds of the leaves.

"When we first kissed it was to the sound of water in the fountain."

"You're a Naiad," I said.

"What's a Naiad?"

"A nymph of the waters."

I had never seen a girl pee, or take a bath.

We went shopping, determined to bathe together if it took all day. It seemed important.

Part Three

I I

The next three days were spent concertedly on school problems. We worked out a complicated curriculum for Sarah. We got tools, supplies, books, drafting equipment, money, and battled the French bureaucracy. Sarah cabled and wrote her trustee about the change in her plans. In the course of getting some books for a survey course in English literature which Sarah was to take, we saw Lady Sybil in the English bookstore. She was one of the great English novelists of the day, much photographed and painted, a center of controversy, friend or enemy of most of the great living writers, many painters, and composers. She had been legendary since I could remember such things. We took Sarah's books to Micini, to whom Lady Sybil was talking, to get them checked out. That accomplished, Lady Sybil said to us. "You two are coming to have tea with me," and set off for the door. We followed, unquestioningly.

She was tall, oval-faced, narrow-shouldered, wide-hipped, and was dressed in a full-skirted purple costume which accentuated her remarkable shape, topped by a purple toque with a purple feather. Her total effect was theatrical and compelling. In the arcade she asked Sarah, "Would you please show me your sketchbook?"

Sarah handed it to her. We walked in silence as she turned the pages, looking at each carefully. I hoped it did not contain any studies of my genitals. It didn't. Finished, she said, with great satisfaction, "Good."

The word seemed to me not to be applied to the sketches. Rather it had something to do with Lady Sybil. Her apartment was off the Avenue in a beautiful court-yard, with its own separate entrance. At the door she stopped, immobile, silent. It had a marvelous polished brass knocker. Nothing seemed to be about to happen. I asked, "Shall I knock?"

"Why not ring the bell?"

"Because I want to touch the knocker."

"You're a romantic."

I rang the bell knowing that she was going to give me a very hard time. A small dark plump Martinican let us in, obviously a privileged companion rather than a maid. Lady Sybil's apartment, like her clothes and her companion, had an almost theatrical regality. The walls, at that time, were covered with large vivid sketches by the Italian painter Peresutti, for the sets and costumes of a ballet by Stravinsky. Sarah was entranced. We talked about them until the Martinican brought tea, sat down, and served it. Lady Sybil asked me, "Have you read *The Sun Also Rises?*"

"Yes. I love it."

"What is it about?"

"Love and despair."

"Give me the plot."

"Really?"

"Yes, in full."

"Jake, an American newspaper correspondent in Paris, and Lady Brett, an English aristocrat, are in love. She had been a VAD during the war. He had been emasculated by a bullet, in a plane in Italy. She had nursed him, in London, afterwards. As the novel opens they are both in despair because they cannot consummate their love. She is about to marry Mike, a bankrupt, burned-out Scotchman of rich but uncertain antecedents, and she is also playing with a rich Greek-American Count, named Mippipopolous, in an amusing, sophisticated way. Jake introduces her to Robert Cohen, a well-off Jewish-American writer of sorts, whom everyone in the novel dislikes. He has had training as a boxer. He leaves his possessive mistress, Frances, and goes off with Lady Brett for two weeks, I can't remember exactly how long. Bill, a marvelously funny American writer, appears, to go to the fiesta at Pamplona and to go fishing with Jake. Lady Brett, Mike, and Robert Cohen join them in Pamplona. Lady Brett, who is thirty-four, is smitten by Romero, a nineteen-year-old matador. Things become very strained. Finally Robert Cohen knocks down Mike and Jake and beats up Romero. Lady Brett and Romero go to Madrid together. She soon decides to give him up, however, before she hurts him or is herself hurt. She telephones Jake, who goes to her rescue. That's the end. There are some other, minor characters who don't count."

"You forgot to mention that Lady Brett is a drunk and a trollop."

"True, but terribly attractive. She is torn by love and despair."

"And that all of these characters, with the exception of Robert Cohen, are smashed most, if not all, of the time."

"Also true. Jake, Mike, and Robert are put in despair by their love for Lady Brett, each in a different way. Bill just drinks on general principles."

"Why is a drunken trollop who has three men in despair so attractive?"

"Because she is haunted by her love for Jake."

"Why then does she not fall to and love him?"

"Because he is emasculated."

"Why should that matter?"

"They are both overcome by the enormity of his loss."

"Surely, with a little ingenuity, he could satisfy her carnal desires."

This came as an appalling idea to me. I did not know exactly what she meant, and thought I was going to fail the examination.

"Do buck up," she said. "Sex is overrated. If he had lost both hands but kept his privy parts, would the relationship have been different?"

"I would think so, but still tragic. She is not drawn as a person who wants to nurse, in spite of the VAD. She wants to *be* nursed. Jake nurses her."

"Jake refuses to satisfy her and watches, oozing self-pity, while she indulges in kittenish pranks with a dreadful American businessman cum Count, a pathetic American Jew, a vacuously brutal Scotchman, and a nineteen-year-old in tight pants. What does that make him?"

"A rather hollow man, granted, but then he has been grievously wounded. I feel that his emasculation is meant to be symbolic."

"Then why not *make* it symbolic? Why have his missing privy parts a personage in the cast of characters?"

I began to feel desperate. To me the book was the quintessence of romantic *angst*, and she was tearing that to shreds. I noticed that Sarah, on the edge of her seat, had lapsed into one of her Serene Beauty trances, which indicated that she was nervous.

"Because that would take away the inevitability of the relationship. The damage cannot be repaired."

"Can psychic damage be repaired, in spite of Mister Freud? Let me read you something." She took the book out from under the tea table, opened it at a bookmark, and said, "Bill says, 'You don't work. One group claims women support you. Another group claims you're impotent.'

" 'No,' I said, 'I just had an accident.'

" 'Never mention that,' Bill said. 'That's the sort of thing that can't be spoken of. That's what you ought to work up into a mystery, like Harry's bicycle.'

"It's too bad that he didn't take his own advice, don't you think?" Lady Sybil asked.

"You're hurting my feelings. But I suppose you're right. If Hemingway had not set the situation up, in the beginning, as inevitable, the book would have had greater dimensions. But could he also have achieved that kind of glamor, which makes it so compelling, at least to me?"

"You *are* a romantic. Why do you think Bill is so marvelously funny?"

We talked about each character. When we came to Count Mippipopolous I discovered that Lady Sybil was very anti-American. She believed in him as a type, naively. My brain felt tired. I wanted to end that mayhem. I asked her, very seriously, "Did you know that at Miami Beach, in Florida, the Chamber of Commerce has constructed a huge electrically lit moon, on a barge? Every night they tow it over the horizon, so that lovers on the beach can love, regardless of the real moon's phases. They shut it off at midnight on Saturday, of course, and turn it on again at midnight Sunday."

"You rascal," she said, laughing. "Where do you live?"
She wrote it down in a large address book.

"You, little Rascal, and you, little Nympha, must come
and see me again soon. I have plans for you. I will leave a
note at your hotel. And don't stop thinking about *The Sun
Also Rises*."

We said our goodbyes and left. I felt exhausted. Sarah
said, "You passed, little cretin, but now what?"

"We'll have to wait and see."

"Where do I fit in?"

"I don't know, but I have a feeling that you will."

"I have a feeling I won't. She scares me to death. Power-
ful intellectual woman are not my cup of tea. I don't know
how to cope with them."

"I suppose I like them, though they make me tired, because I'm used to the type. My mother is one, and so is my
grandmother, my father's mother."

"You haven't talked to your mother since the day we
met, have you?"

"No."

"Are you going to tell her about us?"

"Yes."

"Why?"

"Because she'll find out anyway."

"The thought scares me. What will she think? Will she
make a fuss?"

"I don't think so. She introduced us, after all. She must
have foreseen that there might be consequences."

"I hope, for my sake, that she takes it calmly. I don't
want to be the cause of your scrapping. I wouldn't know
how to behave."

"Don't worry."

"When are you going to tell her?"

"The next time she checks up on me, which should be very soon. I'm not going to go to her with the information."

"Those Peresutti drawings were really marvelous. When I saw them I had the feeling of being at home, at last."

"Why don't you see if you can study with him?"

"Because I want to study with you."

"Don't be silly!"

"I'm not. I know of an awful lot of things I can do. Perhaps, in the vacuum of a classical education, they will come out faster and more truly than with a sort of genius like Peresutti. I want to struggle along with you, my true love."

At my hotel the *concierge* handed me a *pneumatique* from my mother. It was as if we had conjured it up: She wrote:

Dearest one, I have not seen or heard from you in weeks. I feel deprived. Do call me when you get this. I want to know how you are—what you are doing—all your news. M.

It made me feel uneasy. I gave it to Sarah and set off for the Post Office, cutting across the square, to phone. On the way I counted the days of our love. Fourteen. Well, technically my mother was right. Two weeks *are* plural. Friday answered. After an appropriate amount of kidding around he said, "I'll call Madame."

Pause.

"Oh, my darling, you're so kind. How are you?"

"Fine."

"Are you *really* all right?"

"Yes."

"What are you doing?"

"Talking to *you*, Mother."

"I can't wait until you grow up. You'll be marvelous. I just hope I'll live to see the day. Have you seen Sarah again?"

"Yes."

"How much?"

"All the time."

"Have you slept with her?"

"Yes."

"Is it good?"

"Yes."

"In the name of the Lord . . . !" now thoroughly exasperated.

"I love you, Mother, but oh that kid!"

"Thank God!" she shrieked, nearly deafening me. "Did she tell you?"

"Yes."

"I knew she would. She really had no alternative."

"Why didn't *you* tell me?"

"What! Are you crazy! If I had, you would have run like a wild hare."

Pause.

"Isn't that so?"

"Yes."

"Well, why don't you thank me?"

"Thank you, Mother."

"You're absolutely, totally, impossibly impossible. When does school start?"

"The day after tomorrow."

"Is everything all set?"

"Yes."

"Is Sarah going to go to school here?"

"Yes."

"Is everything all set for her too?"

"Yes."

"My darling, you *are* wonderful. Will the two of you come to tea tomorrow? I long to see you both."

"We'd love to."

"Five o'clock," she said and hung up.

I walked back under the arcade, slowly, mad at my mother. Even if she did hand me Sarah, need she be nosey? Even talk about it at all? No! I opened the door to my room, finding Sarah, nude, working at my drafting board.

"What if I'd been my waiter?"

"Well, I daresay you would have been pleased but not surprised."

I sighed.

"That isn't the thing troubling you. Tell me what happened with your mother."

I told her. She said, "She's really something, isn't she?"

"She really is."

"But, you know, it's more funny than anything else."

"I suppose so."

"Did you irritate her on purpose?"

"I suppose so. I get that way when she pushes me."

"You know, your mother loves you intelligently. My mother doesn't. You can't imagine the difference."

"You've told me really nothing about your mother. I'd love to know about her. I want to be able to picture her."

"All right."

She flipped over a page in her sketchbook and started to draw. I took off my clothes and lay on my stomach the

77

wrong way on the bed, watching her. The sketch finished, she looked at it once, critically, got up, pulled the curtains, darkening the room, sat on the bed and handed it to me.

"That's what she looks like."

She then told me a tale of such deprivation, insensitivity, and unconscious cruelty that after a while I began to cry for her, my love.

"You shouldn't be the one to cry. I should. But I can't. I haven't cried for years," she said, and began licking my tears away.

"Lovely salt tears," she said.

Tea at my mother's the next day was tremendous fun. She told us, among other things, that she was making plans to take us to certain plays, the Opera, and the Russian Ballet. We discussed alternatives. Sarah was delighted. I knew we would go in style. As we left, my mother suddenly turned to Sarah, asking, "Does he still cry a lot?"

"Yes."

"Oh—Mother!"

"Don't 'Oh—Mother' me, my pet. If I had asked *you*, you would simply have said 'Oh—Mother.' "

My mother disliked the expression of emotions. She wanted them muted, pianissimo, if at all.

"He's always been that way," she went on, "born near a brook. I hope you can persuade him to stop, if only in public. I tried, and failed. It would give me such pleasure if we could go to a sad play together without tears. Also, it's part of growing up. Stiff upper lip, and all that!"

We laughed, but she had made me angry. Going down in the gilded cage I shook my head madly. Sarah asked, "Do you love Brahms?"

"No. My mother has forbidden it."

She lunged at me, pinned me against the grating, grabbed it with both hands and squeezed me against it with all her might. I began to laugh. On the sidewalk, she said, "I love your tears. Never stop. You must teach me to cry again, too. Then we can cry together. It will make us happy."

Halfway to the square I told her, "I feel as if I lived in a tiny open airplane cockpit flying in a huge damp mother cloud, going quite fast, but never fast enough to get out of it."

"Don't think about it so much—then it will go away. Think about me."

She tilted her face. We strolled along, kissing lovingly, until we bumped into a large woman in mourning. She snarled at us. I apologized. We started to walk very fast. At her hotel we ran up the stairs to her room, slammed the door, tore off our clothes. She was first on the bed. I jumped on her.

12

School started. I soon discovered that Sarah was a ferocious worker, a born designer, knew no formal perspective, no grammar, did not know how to be taught, and was morosely enthralled by the experience. She made school seem fresh again for me.

She was frequently blocked. She had not learned to give up unsatisfactory concepts quickly, in favor of random alternatives. When she did give up she threw her sketches away, instead of saving them for reference, then often began again where she had left off—punishing herself. Nor had she learned to solve problems in parts, recognizing them as parts, in preparation for a new attack on the whole. She would save them and attempt to make a whole, in an agony of frustration. When she could not unravel intellectual or graphic tangles reasonably quickly, she rose into silent, towering rages at herself. They paralyzed her for long periods of time, wasting it and breaking the flow of our love. In one, she withdrew from me, and I from her, defensively.

I learned to forestall them by helping her with the block, when I knew she was in one. At first, when she was deeply in, it took several separate steps, spaced out, to release her. Later, a generalization would do. But I sometimes did not know, or could not help. She was impatient, self-critical, self-destructive.

I learned to dispel her rages by an experiment. Sarah was

very breast-conscious. Her clothes revealed them, she often brushed them against me and, when we were alone, touched them unconsciously. They were, mysteriously, a part of her *me*. In one of her rages, instead of leaving her alone I walked up behind her, seized her breasts, squeezed her nipples and pressed. She put her head back on my chest. I propelled her to a chair, sat her on my lap, and continued to press. She sighed, put her head on my shoulder, and subsided.

"You're fructiferous," I said.

"What does that mean?"

"Fruit-bearing."

"It sounds sexy. Do you suppose I will have fruit flies in my old age?"

"I expect so. They're cute, you know."

"You're an angel. I can go back to work now. But first let's fuck."

She went back, grimly, but able to cope.

Her equilibrium recovered, I could try to help with the block which had caused the rage. If I could, I discovered that to leave the room for a short time helped her. She needed a little loneliness then. I would go for a walk or go see the cook.

The day came for Old Stroph's critique of my first problem. We walked toward my school, Sarah's sketchbook under her arm. After a while I put my arm around her, hugged her, and said, "This may be a trying experience. Gird yourself."

"Why?"

"After a crit the students are at their worst. They go berserk."

"What do they do?"

"They pick on somebody to haze. Today it will probably be you, because they haven't seen you before."

"Brouhaha?"

"Yes, but no violence. The one thing you don't do is sock people. However, you can throw bits of dried clay metopes at the bicycle cops, on certain occasions."

"Have you done that?"

"Yes, but not to hit them. I've also socked a guy."

"Will there be any other girls there?"

"A few. Shopgirls, part-time tarts, hangers-on of the students. In a better world they might be students themselves."

"Like me?"

She made me feel miserable.

"Yes. They will assume you're one of them."

The approach to the great exhibition hall, through courtyards and loggias, was so overpoweringly classical that we fell silent, awed by our ability to penetrate the school's matrix, on foot. We dawdled, Sarah enthralled, me eager and reluctant. The hall itself, high, elaborately coffered, pilastered, marble-floored, was filled with orderly rows of portable display panels, without spaces between them, forming generous aisles. The drawings were hung on them, side by side, in rank order, clockwise, from best to worst. A jury of professors, with help from porters, had spent the last three days arranging it. The students were thinly spread out, mostly alone, agonizing or gloating over their place in the hierarchy. The atmosphere was muted, silent, quick handshakes, whispers, and occasional uncouth clacks of metal-tipped heels on the marble floor. The huge volume of the hall seemed to soak up sounds, mediocrity, people. Still, it was a moment of truth, as truth was then known.

Sarah and I separated, going around in opposite directions, meeting halfway, passing as conspirators, meeting all the way around.

"I found yours," she whispered. "It looks great."

We went to look at it. The Chief of our *Atelier* came in to round us up in front of the highest-ranked drawings, so obscenely that I felt besmeared. He was an expert at making one feel like that. Old Stroph came in, mustachioed, fat, pompous, harassed, ready to blow us up. He stood, back to the drawings, our group in a thick ring around him, and began: "A catastrophe, my poor children."

He summarized what we should have done, why we had, without exception, failed, and, in conclusion, urged us, in the future, to take his advice to the letter, in order to avoid catastrophes such as we had brought on ourselves in this instance. I had heard it all before but nevertheless enjoyed his delivery, particularly the dramatic crescendo of the conclusion. At the same time I determined to take his advice with even less regularity than I had in the past.

He then moved along the line of drawings, commenting, comparing, criticizing, and making suggestions. The group oozed along with him. When he got to mine, Sarah grabbed my elbows from behind and hung on, invisible to him, behind my back, beyond the outer circle. My drawing, both in technique and intent, was alien to anything else in the room. I could feel the surge of anticipation in those around me. He went at it, sarcastic, unbelieving, as if it were supposed to be a recreation of a nineteenth-century stereotype, ending up, predictably unpredictable, with: "But keep it up."

There were discreet titters. After a few more drawings I had had enough. I knew he would go faster and faster as he went along, ending up at a trot. Sarah and I would need protection at the café, later, where we all went to discuss grades, ideas, and his remarks. I sought out two friends of mine to ask them to sit with us at a table for four. One, my dear Polish-Russian friend Pytor Piatagorsky, nicknamed Pee Pee. The other, a Frenchman whose first name was Claude, followed by five names, the last of which was that of one of the great families of France. He was nicknamed Anonymous.

Pytor had been through his military service, had left for a while, and had been through various emotional vicissitudes. He was an enormously talented, gloomy type.

Claude was eighteen. We had been in school together. He had a thin, open, expressive face, and reminded me always of a thoroughbred horse. His sister, Monique, who was twenty, I considered an older woman, but liked her very much, nevertheless. In fact if one liked one, one had to like the other, because they were so much alike. Their mother was a reigning beauty and patron of the arts.

Having found them both and explained, I looked for Sarah and found her sketching in a corner. I took her arm, and we left on tiptoe.

The café was nearly empty. We took a table for four and talked about Old Stroph's criticisms of my drawing. Pytor and Claude came in together. I introduced Sarah and ordered coffee. Our fellow students arrived in a noisy mass. They surrounded us, all talking at once.

"Who is she, Tic Toc? Why haven't you brought her before?"

Tic Toc was my nickname, short for Alarm Clock, signifying someone who tics along quietly and then suddenly causes alarm.

"What's her name?"

"Sarah," I said.

"Sarah!" they yelled at the top of their lungs.

"Is she foreign?"

Everyone talked at once.

"Sarah is a French name."

"No, it's Jewish. She eats cooked babies."

"Look at her tits."

"They're more like automobile headlights."

"She puts them on with spirit gum."

"She's too small for a good fuck."

"How do you manage, Tic Toc?"

"Tic Toc, has she got a cunt, or only one hole down there?"

"She's got two, but her cunt's been sewn up."

"Then Tic Toc must fuck her ass."

"Down with Tic Toc, he's a dirty sodomizing foreigner."

Someone, lightning-fast, grabbed Sarah's sketchbook from her lap. He flipped through it and suddenly screamed, "Tic Toc's balls!"

Pandemonium. Everyone yelled, "Tic Toc's balls!"

The girls let out periodic piercing shrieks. Several students grabbed for the sketchbook, its pages were torn out and handed around. Everyone scuffled. The pages were finally torn into small pieces and flung in the air. The noise was deafening. Sarah looked serenely beautiful, unmoved, untouched.

When things calmed down we started to discuss the exhibition. Then a tattoo of loud remarks erupted over the general buzz of conversation, an obscene litany.

"She pisses 'Whiskey and Soda.'"

"Tic Toc drinks it."

"She fucks herself with a whole loaf of bread."

"Tic Toc eats it."

"She menstruates red wine."

"Tic Toc drinks it."

"She farts Guerlain."

"Tic Toc gets a hard on."

"She farts tear gas."

"Tic Toc cries."

We could not talk. Sarah had the picture. I put the money on the table. The room hushed. Sarah and I got up. Dead silence. Pytor said, "My dear friend, I would love to meet beautiful Sarah someday."

"You shall. Come to breakfast on Sunday morning at nine. You come too, Claude, and bring Monique."

"Till Sunday."

"Till Sunday."

Sarah gave them a dazzling smile. Claude gave us a chagrined grimace. When we got to the door there was a sudden deafening chorus of boos, jeers, manic laughter, girl-shrieks, farts, pounding, foot-stamping, and squeaks. We had walked only a short way toward the *quai* when we heard running footsteps behind us. One of the boys whirled in front of us, crouched, flapped his arms, and moved his pelvis like a copulating monkey. Between exaggerated panting, he said, "Sarah, Sarah, give me your sketchbook again. I haven't seen any pornography in a week. Fuck me—fuck me. You too, Tic Toc. Both of you fuck me. If I had two cocks I'd fuck you both at once. Gladly, gladly."

I pushed him down, gently, on the sidewalk, where he writhed. As we started off again I was careful to step on his fingers. A few seconds later he went running past, in his monkey crouch, rocking from side to side, flapping his arms, and turned a corner. When we got there he was walking soberly away.

We came to the *quai*, crossed the street, and walked along the bookstalls, silent. Suddenly, explosively, Sarah said, "My God! Is it always like that?"

"Always. Sometimes worse."

"How could it be worse?"

"Scenes in the *Atelier*. Your pants taken down, glue smeared on your nates. Systematic thievery. Systematic persecution of one person at a time. Enforced labor for those who are older. They range up to thirty-five."

"Why?"

"To make as many as possible fall into the lowest common denominator."

"Has all that happened to you?"

"Yes."

"Why did you put up with it?"

"At first there seemed no alternative."

"Why did you sock the guy? Because of the glue?"

"Not specifically. In a quiet moment I picked a chum at random, warned him, and let him have it, on general principles."

"What did he do?"

"Cried."

"Because you hit him so hard?"

"Oh, no. I didn't hit him that hard. I didn't have to. He cried because he was involved in a disgraceful incident. One simply does not sock people. Anything but that. By the same token one does not get socked."

"What next? He's crying. Is he on the floor?"

"Yes. He sat on the floor and wiped his tears with his knuckles. I took off my shirt and looked for trouble. Everyone gathered around us in a circle saying, 'Tsk, Tsk, you shouldn't have done that, Fife.' Fife was my nickname then, short for 'Five o'clock tea.' The boy I had socked got up and left altogether. The Chief asked me to put on my shirt and wait in the shop, worried and polite for the first and only time in my experience. There was a lengthy meeting in the drafting room. A committee came into the shop. They explained, as to a naughty child, the heinousness of my crime, the purity of their motives, the efficacy of the system. I explained to them that I would not be badgered any more, that I'd sock anyone who tried, and that every time I was stolen from I would pick someone's tools, at random, and break them up.

"They explained to me that in that case I could only be construed as a 'Wild Beast Foreigner,' that I would not be welcome in the affairs of the students, and that no one would nigger for me. That was exactly what I wanted. The meeting ended with warnings that if I told Old Stroph anything about it, they would be forced to take more drastic steps. And that, my love, accounts for my present blissful freedom.

"I worried about Claude and Pytor, particularly Claude. I had, of course, put them in a difficult position. But as it turned out I was quickly accepted as a special phenomenon. I'm really on more friendly terms with most of them than I was before."

"What else?"

"Group visits to brothels, designed to elevate the truly obscene types, harass the exhibitionists, and reinforce the commonality, the types who go through it all with their underwear on."

"Tell me about it?"

I did.

"When you told me, that first day of ours, about your school, you only sketched in all this. I should have asked you more questions."

"I thought you would be shocked."

"Doesn't it mean that you will have to go somewhere else for sustenance?"

"Sooner or later."

"Why not sooner?"

"Because I'm not quite through here yet. After all, I've barely begun. There must be something to it."

"We could go to London, Rome, New Haven."

"When I go, it occurs to me, I'm going to America."

"It's settled then?"

"I guess so. Isn't it odd?"

"No. Will you go to Harvard or Yale or someplace like that?"

"I really haven't thought about it. M. I. T. keeps crossing my mind."

"Have you talked to your mother about this?"

"Not really."

"Will she mind?"

"I don't think so. She has the farm. She believes in decisiveness and magic. She will accept whatever I decide as a surefire magic formula. Also, it occurs to me, she accepts divisiveness."

"What do you mean?"

"She leads several lives, separately—social, intellectual,

French, American, country, solitary—her lovers. She doesn't need to mix them."

"You forget that you are one of her nine lives. Probably the only important one."

"Yes, but I share with the others, share and share alike."

"Does that make you jealous?"

"Yes, sometimes. Sometimes it's a relief."

"You're not like that."

"No. I like *bouillabaisse*."

"Like our life together. Love, sex, work, games, in a dreamlike amalgam. I don't think many people can lead that sort of life, just as a practical matter. We can do it here, in this framework, but could we do it anywhere else?"

"I don't know," I said and plunged into misery, knowing that the real answer was almost surely no. I guided her to a stall. We fingered books with our free hands. I felt her miserable too. We started strolling again. After a while she said, again explosively, "What about the café?"

"*What* about it?"

"Your friend Pytor humiliated them for us. Did you ask him for breakfast simply to reinforce that?"

"Yes. And no. You don't know yet what a joy a day with the three of them can be. You have a lovely experience in store, for a change."

"What about your French friend, Claude? I got no sense of him."

"He was humiliated, as a Frenchman, too soon today. He froze. He's very aware."

"Like you. What about that last weird boy?"

"I don't know. It's hard to say. I suppose he is locked up

in the French boy-nightmare. They are being poorly educated for a world that never was. They are the slaves of
their system, will remain so, and underneath, know it.
Only Claude and Pytor, of that group, will escape, because
they are talented, rich, and well connected. We know we
have opportunities, even great opportunities in our future.
They know they don't. I sometimes think of it as self-
protection. If your peaks are low, the mean has to be very
low. Despair must have limits."

"I don't want to go there again."

"Once is educational and instructive. Twice verges on
self-punishment."

"No wonder you're tender as in 'ouch.' It's so nice for
me that you're also tender as in 'loving care.' "

We strolled along rummaging in the quaiside bookstalls
that we had been parralleling on our walk. I saw Lady
Sybil some distance ahead, doing the same thing. She saw
us. I waved. She cut me dead. Sarah had not seen her. I
considered crossing the street, thought better of it, and said
to Sarah, "Lady Sybil is coming. Don't look at her. When
I squeeze your arm start walking and kissing me."

When Lady Sybil was close enough I squeezed Sarah
and we started kissing, almost a parody of lovers. Lady
Sybil swept straight at us. We all stopped, a pace apart.
She said, "Spoil sports! But I have driven you to a frenzy
of defensive osculation."

Laughing, I wondered what she would try next. She
went on, "Come and have tea with me. I want you to help
me rearrange the furniture."

I felt slightly miffed, but game. As we started tea, she
started an acute, fascinating analysis of Joyce's "Work in

Progress." We were spellbound. I began to see her as a solid core of scholarship surrounded by a dazzling nimbus of playful creativity.

Tea concluded, she told us that she was giving a dinner party that night, named and gave us a short, vicious, uncanny description of each invited guest, most of whom we knew of. I shuddered to think what ours would sound like. There were, however, two exceptions, which gave me hope. Her brother's was kind. Peresutti's was vicious but romantic. She asked, "What, do you think, can be done with them?"

We discussed that intensely, guessing how they would react to each other, what combinations would produce the most fireworks, what topics might catalyze, how they should be seated, during and after dinner, in order to produce the most friction. Sarah was much amused. Lady Sybil was planning a play for unwitting actors.

As we left she said, "As we are in cahoots, you must come to tea tomorrow, to find out how well this plan succeeded."

On our way back, Sarah said, "You like her, don't you?"

"Yes. She's amusing."

"She's a lady, isn't she?"

"Yes, very much so. To the manner born."

"But she's also a vicious bitch."

"Yes. I can't imagine being at ease around Lady Sybil. She's too bright and too scary."

"How can a lady be a bitch?"

"They're not incompatible. Think of Lady Brett."

"It's funny," she said.

13

Sunday morning, at dawn, we were wakened by a knock on my door. Half asleep, naked, I got up and opened it a crack. Claude and Pytor were there. I opened it wide, delighted.

"Comrades! But why so early?"

We shook hands. Claude said, "We've been up all night talking. We got going around and around in circles, getting more depressed each time. I tried to wake up Monique, but she wouldn't. She'll be here later though."

I put my hands on their chests to keep them where they were, and went to the armoire to get something for Sarah to put on, saying, "Go on."

"We thought that seeing you would cheer us up. Or that you would get things so confused that even a vicious circle would look like a tetrahedron."

I found a small, fuzzy pink sweater, took it to Sarah, helped her on with it, and gave her a warm wet kiss, holding her breasts. I wanted her to remember me.

"Actually," Pytor said, "we'd settle for a vicious ellipse."

"What got you started?"

"Old Stroph. Who else could cause such anguish?"

"My mother says 'A little misinformation is good for a growing boy.'"

"But Old Stroph is a mine of misinformation."

"Maybe a lot is better than a little."

"It's so depressing."

I went to the door and propelled them around the corner to the bed. Claude squeezed into the alcove, took Sarah's hand and kissed it. Her expression told me that she had never had that done before, and was delighted. Then Pytor, and more delight. Claude climbed over the foot of the bed and sat on the window sill, wedged in between the jambs. He picked up one of Sarah's sketchbooks and a pencil, flipped a page, and began a sketch of the theater's arcade, the sketchbook propped against his knees. I got into bed again. Pytor sat facing us, on its foot, his legs crossed, his head near the alcove's low ceiling. Claude's pencil made scratching sounds, his aquiline face was intent. He said, "Did you know that Pytor worked for our beloved *Patron* last summer?"

"Yes," I said, "and I'm dying to hear about it. Tell us, Pytor."

I felt filled with bliss. Hours to spend with my most dearly beloved and my two dear friends. I had a mad impulse to kiss them all, or to cry. They looked marvelous in the poses they had taken. They glowed in the low pink light of dawn, reflected back from the façade of the theater, Claude in silhouette, rimmed with light. Sarah's fuzzy pink sweater, red on the shadow side, looked the essence of warmth. Her face was at its most receptive, her large dark eyes, her marvelous full mouth spoke her eagerness, her long black hair was mussed, enchantingly, her hands were clasped on top of the covers, as if to keep herself in. I ached with love for her. Pytor began, "Old Stroph told me to report at the office one day at nine. The office hours are from eight to twelve and two to six. I was terribly nervous, wondering how I would do in the real world. I got there at half-past eight, determined to show my eagerness, if I had nothing else to offer. The office Chief told me to come back at eleven. 'Don't worry,' he said, 'You will be paid.' I got back at eleven sharp, having sweated out the intervening time, somehow. The Chief gave me a small drawing, to trace. I went at it as hard as I could, and had it finished at twelve. I told the Chief, as he was leaving for lunch, that it was finished. He said, 'What! Are you going to do all the work in this office? What will the rest of us do? We have to live, too, you know. We'll call this a day's work. Don't come back until four. The *Patron* never gets in before then. You can read books the rest of the afternoon. And I advise you to have a little consideration for others.' "

He paused.

"My first day's work."

Sarah said, "Featherbedding. How does he make any money?"

"I don't know, really. But he makes enough to buy books. The next day the Chief told me 'I'm going to put you in charge of answering the door. When book salesmen come, turn them away. If the *Patron* is here, be smart about it. Don't let him catch you or he'll fire us all. He has a mania for books and book salesmen.' The whole office is lined with books, floor to ceiling, and there are piles of them everywhere, on the floor, tables, chairs, everywhere. Very few of them have been read. I cut pages as I read, all summer long."

"It's a fine art," Claude said, "provided you approach it with passion and reverence."

"One day Old Stroph called me into his office. I was alarmed, thinking he was going to blow me up, or fire me, for not doing enough work. He told me there was no more room for books in the office, that his wife would not allow any more in the apartment, and told me to hide all new books behind the old ones. 'How will you find them?' I asked. 'Make a list,' he said. So then I hid books. 'Dust them while you're at it,' the Chief told me. So then I dusted. Two or three salesmen came every day. I met a rather seedy segment of the working public in that way."

"Wasn't it awfully boring?" I asked.

"No. Strangely enough it was rather fun. He is unselective in his purchases—catholic, I should say."

"What did you like best?"

"The Italians, Palladio, Scammozzi, and some books on the Italian gardens. Did you know, Sarah, that some were conceived as theaters, or more accurately, as settings for performances?"

"No. I must look into that. What fun."

"Anyway, the office was working on some new buildings for the École Polytechnique. In an agonizingly slow crescendo the design got finished and sent off to my father's office, where everything else was to be done. We cleaned up and the Chief gave all of us the next day off. When we got back the drawings were back again too. Old Stroph and the Chief were in frantic conference. They had forgotten the toilets. In fact there was no plumbing at all, or any place to put it.

"The building was a uniformly wide structure around an irregular courtyard. The bays were all alike. The staircases were in the corners. The bays were supposed to allow classrooms, or laboratories or drafting rooms, as the school staff decided. There didn't seem to be any place for offices, and no partitions were shown. It was just a big senseless

loft. The Chief and Old Stroph tucked the toilets in next
to the staircases, causing half bays, and of course screwing
up the elevations. 'The half bays will be good for odd things
like janitors,' Old Stroph said, oozing self-satisfaction."

"What did your father say about it?" I asked.

"Nothing. I didn't mention it, and neither did he."

"Why not?" Claude asked.

"Well, he may not have known about it, and anyway
he's Olympian, at least with me. He's very hard to get at
these days. You may think of the great Professor Piatagorsky as thrilling, bubbling with ideas, but believe me, at
home he's not."

"You must be underrating him."

"Perhaps. But I can't imagine studying with him, I suppose because he's my father. Anyway, one day the Chief
told me to block in a perspective of a bank building in
Algiers. It's in a phony Moroccan style. 'That will be a
week's work,' he said. I did it in two days and went back
to my other duties, such as cutting pages. A week later Old
Stroph came in saying, 'Is the perspective blocked in yet?'
He's apparently completely taken in by his Chief. He
looked at it and said, 'It's ugly, isn't it?' The Chief said,
'No, *Patron*, it's just the angle it's taken from.' He had
told me the angle to use. 'Get me things,' Old Stroph told
him. The Chief spread tracing paper over my drawing, put
tools and things on the board. Old Stroph looked at it for
a long time, then put his head on his arms on the board,
and fell asleep. The Chief motioned us to stop working and
make no sound. We all got out books and were careful not
to make sounds turning the pages. When he woke up,
about an hour later, he told me to stand by his side 'just

there' and the Chief to stand by his other side, 'just there.' Then he made a really beautiful free-hand perspective. When it was blocked in and some indications of detail added, he whammed it with his palm, making us all jump, and said to the Chief, 'Make it look like that.' They started all over again. The Chief wouldn't let me take the free-hand drawing and work it backwards. 'We will intuit it,' he said."

"Tell them about the duel," Claude said, handing the sketchbook to Sarah, who started a sketch of him, in the window.

"Wait," I said, "first would you open the door so my waiter will come in as soon as he starts stirring about. Aren't you hungry?"

"Yes. Ravenous."

Prytor opened the door and started in on another and yet another incredible tale. My waiter came in, obviously intrigued. I ordered quantities of coffee, croissants, and jam. When he came back he served us all slowly, with great care, and left, leaving the door open. I was sure that he wanted to listen to what Claude would have to say. He revered The Nobility. The room filled with the smells of hot coffee, hot milk, and hot pastry. We talked of the practice of architecture, as revealed by Old Stroph, until it was time to get ready for Monique. Claude and Prytor went to the W. C.'s, Sarah and I got dressed and made the bed.

Monique came in rapidly, shook hands rapidly, introduced herself to Sarah before I could, took her arm and led her to the window seat. Her perfume was heavenly, perfect for her. They knelt on the seat, arms on the sill, their heads in the open window, their bottoms and hair lovely. My waiter gave Monique her breakfast in rapture

—female nobility—almost too much for him. The room filled again with the marvelous smells of food.

Monique was tall for a Frenchwoman, thin, always beautifully dressed. Her homely face had a vivacity which made her extraordinarily attractive. She was a linguist, a pacifist, and was going to the school of diplomacy. Claude and Monique were so alike that they knew instinctively how both to support and to hurt each other. Monique was the more aggressive and critical of the two. Claude was often mad at her. Their fireworks were engaging, the froth on a profoundly close relationship. When she had finished breakfast Claude asked her, "Do you feel you know anything?"

"Yes. Four languages."

"That's knowing tools. What can you do with them, except translate?"

"Grasp more firmly what other peoples feel. Make comparisons. They're useful you know. They can, I should think, even be the base for something creative."

Claude turned to me.

"Do you feel you know anything?"

"Practically nothing. Nothing practical in my case. I imitate things others have done, don't like my imitations, and don't know what to do about it. Something is missing. It worries me all the time."

"How do you know when you know something?"

"Personal things? By confiding."

"That's so intimate."

"Why not? I imagine that the most intimate experience one can have is to be in touch with one's creativity. If I had that, I don't think I would need as many things or people as I need now."

"Or confidants?" Monique asked.

"Probably not. When I hear my thought reverberating around in a confiding atmosphere it helps me decide whether or not it is really a part of me, or something I have learned, and am foisting on myself. So if I knew already there would be no point in talking about it."

"But confiding is so difficult. You're always getting put off."

"You have to be lucky," I said.

"He confides in the cook," Sarah said.

"Give me an example," Claude asked.

"Well, I fear and desire self-immolation. That isn't really the right word, though. I don't want to kill myself as a sacrifice, I want to open myself up, to be in an extreme peace, my animality in abeyance. Then perhaps I would understand certain things, love for example, which it keeps obscuring."

"I can see you in a nimbus," Claude said.

"If I told that to my mother she might say, 'Back to the womb, dear? A boy needs his mother, I always say.' If I told that to my cook she might say, 'Psyche was a girl, you know,' which is exactly one of the things I would like to find out about. What it's like."

Monique said, "If I said that to my mother she would say, 'How transcendental of you, dear,' and she would think 'I must do something about Monique soon.'"

Pytor said, "If I said that to Old Stroph he would say, 'My poor boy! What a catastrophe. I feel sorry for you but it's out of my province.'"

Sarah said, "If you said that to your waiter he wouldn't understand at all, but he'd say, 'Have something to eat. It will make you feel better.'"

I said, "If I said that to my father he would probably say, 'That's a useless speculation.' "

Monique asked Sarah, "What would you say if he confided that in you?"

"He did."

"What did you say?"

Sarah blushed, saying, " 'You'd be like the Cheshire Cat.' "

"But that's marvelous! The thing is to enter in, rather than to comment. To be personal. That way you don't make the confidant embarrassed. Do I mean that? Yes I do. The thing is to be *very* personal. To put one's self in the other's shoes. I think of confidants as holding each other in their arms. Somehow, you can't do that with parents. I think I would react as your cook, but would think of the state as being one of pure soul, rather than as a learning process, which you include. So you see you must add me to your list of confidants, my pet."

Claude said to me, "I want to tell you what I think about it."

"Don't. I don't want to hear you. You're sure to be mechanistic. True?"

"True, but you're going to hear it anyway. You see, if you have reduced yourself to a state of pure psyche, have turned out your animal to graze, and want to find out what it's like to be some girl, Monique for example, she most likely would not be in the same state you were in, her animal would be there, yours would come rushing back, and you're through before you've begun. On the other hand, if she was in the same state that you were in, you would only find out about her psyche. So you see, you can't find out about girls that way."

"I shall have to add animal training to the concept."

Pytor said, "Seriously, though, I came perilously close to a state of nonbeing once. It was in the Army. I was assigned as chauffeur to a general stationed in Paris. The only things I was allowed to do on duty were to walk around the car, sit in it, read the manual, wipe it, and look under the bonnet. My general spent most of his time in meetings. I learned to submerge myself in a state of nonbeing. I forced myself into a trance. That trance spread into all my hours, on duty or off. This dawned on me gradually and began to scare me. I decided on an experiment which I hoped would get me transferred, one way or another. I put some oily waste on the engine block and tied some insulated electrical wire over it with thin string. My general came out of his meeting. His aide told me where to go."

Sarah asked, "Did he ever talk to you?"

"No. He told his aide, who told me. When the block heated up, smoke began coming out from under the bonnet. I waited until it was very apparent, then slowed down rapidly, but not so rapidly as to inconvenience my general, jumped out of the car, opened the bonnet, all this very rapidly mind you, reached in, yanked out my contraption, threw it in the gutter, slammed the bonnet shut, jumped into the car, and started off again. My general said, through the speaking tube, 'You are a natural mechanic, my son. Would you like to be transferred to the motor pool?' 'Yes, my general,' I said, and saluted.

"That farce, I think, saved my life, but it took an awfully long time to recover from that state in which one simply wants to cease to exist. You see, I had neither tools nor an existence in theory. I think our troubles with knowing and learning and feeling come because we are taught everything in theory, while buildings, after all, are nothing if not concrete."

Monique asked, "How do you feel, Sarah?"

"I know how to do a lot of small specific things, such as how to make clothes, how to paint scenery, how to take care of props, how to make models. I've never had any theory, and I welcome it, at school, even when the results are ridiculous. So *that's* why it comes out that way! You should be more content with the tools you have, like grammar and mathematics and history, because it seems to me you'll need them to be architects, because of the kind of people you are."

"You're a *me*," I said.

"Have you always been?" Monique asked.

"I don't know. It's hard to tell. I think so."

Claude asked, "And how about you, gentle Pytor. Have you got a *me*?"

"No. I don't think I will have one until I can manipulate concretes according to a held theory, and I can't imagine a held theory until I can manage to slough off the inanities in which we are presently embedded. I feel more destructive than anything else. I don't think I'm a person. I'm an unformed architect."

Claude said, "I feel that I have no contact with reality at all.

" 'Design' is the production of abstract concepts which bear no relation to the facts of twentieth-century life. It's an exercise in beautiful futilities, complete unto itself.

" 'Materials' is meaningless bits and pieces of disparate information, with no clue offered as to how those real things must fit together.

" 'Statics' is abstract, how a beam you've never seen or

felt, can't even imagine, behaves in a laboratory.

" 'History' is an exercise in the creation of hollow models, to emulate and fill—with what?

"What do people really need from buildings? That's never mentioned.

"I can see, say, St. Germain des Prés, as beautiful at certain hours of the day, or in the moonlight, expressive, anachronistic, poverty stricken, but I can't feel the thing itself. I touch it, even hug it. It means nothing. How is it made: I don't really know. Why was it made? I don't know. I'd like to take it apart with my own two hands, to see what it really is. I feel like a Balinese shadow puppet, thin, full of odd-shaped holes, which must fit my missing parts. I'm entirely constructed of theories."

He went, morose, to the record player and put on some dance music by "The Hot Club of France." Sarah and Pytor danced. I danced with Monique, smelling her, unashamedly. Claude changed records and gloomed. We changed partners occasionally. After a while Monique and I sat down on the window seat. She said, "You make me miserable." Then, "Oh don't look so scared, my dear. I'm only jealous of you and Sarah. I have no designs on you. You're not a diplomat, remember?"

"I wish I were."

Monique sometimes began sentences with, "When I catch my diplomat . . ." but I had never believed that she wanted one.

"I take it that this affair of yours will have no ill effects for Sarah?"

"You mean socially? None, I think. She comes from a segment of American life where the social code you were brought up in doesn't exist. And she's very much of an individualist. Psychologically, I suppose we could both be hurt."

"Do you think of marriage?"

"No."

"Does she?"

"I doubt it. We've never discussed it."

"Will you?"

"Come, my dear. We're still exploring."

"When I saw your face this morning I knew that you had made a passage from boy to young man. You used to make me feel like an old lady."

"But Claude didn't?"

"No."

Claude came over, asking, "What are you talking about?"

"You," I said.

"Let me tell you about me. I have several theories. . . ."

I saw my waiter near the door signaling disaster. I went over to him wondering what could bring on such anguish.

"It's the boy all in black," he whispered. "You know, the ho-mo-sex-u-al."

Paul! I went to the door. Paul was standing there, in a state of acute stage fright, his head trembling. I took his arm, led him to the phonograph, took a record he had, and his black homburg, and put them on top of the sideboard.

"Would you like to see my records?"

"Yes," he muttered, and started going through them.

Paul was medium-sized, athletic looking, with a small head and a large face, all rounds—round cheekbones, round dimples, a round mouth in a perpetual smile, even in his then parlous state. He was, as usual, nattily dressed all in black, with black patent leather dancing pumps on his feet.

After a while he said, "I heard music from below and thought you two might be dancing. So I came up. I didn't think you ever entertained."

"This is the first time. Come and meet them."

I introduced him. He kissed Monique's hand formally, Sarah's possessively (she gave me an amused glance) and in a characteristic reversal of form sat cross-legged on my drafting board, all embarrassment gone, talking animatedly, as if he had known Claude, Monique, and Pytor all his life.

"I met these two darlings in the most peculiar way. I dropped into the *bistro* across the square one night, after the theater. They were in a circle of people standing around the taxi driver, at the short end of the bar. Suddenly they popped out of the circle, did a little dance together, and then joined it again. A few minutes later they did the same thing. It was immensely gay and spontaneous and filled me with ideas, waves of them. I wanted to meet them, but I am pathologically shy, or maybe afraid of people, it's dreadful, I have frightful stage fright, even in the chorus line, where I am third from your right at the *Folies-Bergères*, every night except Sunday. You must all come and see me. But where was I? Oh yes. A fare came in looking for the taxi driver, and the circle broke up. These two sat down near me laughing so gaily. It made me sad."

"Why did you do the dance?" Claude asked Sarah.

"The taxi driver was telling a story about Sarah Bernhardt as a fare. He was only concerned with the time he picked her up, the address they went to, the amount of the fare, and unfortunate incidents on the way, with cops and other taxi drivers. Nothing about her. He was deadly serious about it. He must have said 'then' ten thousand times.

We got hysterical, but he's a dear, and we would have hurt his feelings if we had laughed. So when we felt on the verge of erupting we'd clutch each other and dance off. He was unbelievably funny."

Paul went on, "I wanted to meet these two dears desperately, but I couldn't bring myself to go up to them. I went to the *bistro* every day. Finally I found out their names, and realized his mother is a friend of my parents. So I stole one of my father's cards and wrote on it who I was."

"You wrote," I interrupted, "under your father's name, 'A friend of your mother's. I am his son. Paul.'"

Paul's father was a tremendously popular romantic novelist, who was said to have made mints. My mother more or less despised him—"He makes counterfeit mints," she said. Paul went on: "So I gave the card to the taxi driver and asked him to give it to them. They came to the bar, where I was standing, and I suddenly felt all right. We talked about Proust for hours and hours."

He turned to me.

"I did hear music from down below, but really I came to show you the dance you suggested to me that first night. Would you like to see it?"

"We'd love to."

"Sarah, you are going to do it with me, yes?"

"Yes."

"I'll show you first, and then we'll try it, but first let's push this horrid thing in front of the sideboard, so that we can use the diagonal of the room."

Claude and I pushed the drafting board aside while he went to the phonograph and put on his record.

"You four sit on the bed or on the floor in front of it and imagine that the drafting table is a bar with a bunch of working class types in front of it in a knot, who open up to release the dancers, close again, then open up to receive them, and close, hiding them for good."

Monique and Pytor lay on the bed on their stomachs with their chins on their hands. Claude and I sat on the floor, leaning against the footboard.

"The dance is in the form of a T with a short stem and a wide top. Sarah, I'll show you my part first."

He put the pick-up arm on the record he had brought and as the music started suddenly became a man, every vestige of the fairy gone, demonstrating his part intensely, athletically, explaining occasionally. When the music ended he went to the player, a fairy again, saying, "Now Sarah, I'll show you your part."

He put on the music again and instantly became a woman, feminine, fluid, alluring, convincing. I was astonished, and could sense that Claude was too.

"Now do it behind me."

He was more feminine than Sarah. I had been preoccupied with the idea and the nature of her femininity ever since the day we had gone to get her identity card, but solely in terms of her. I now realized, seeing her in contrast with a distillation of the idea, that hers was rooted in her strong sense of self, in her independent spirit and in her creativity, that my mother's was casual, and that Monique's was taut.

And I realized that compared with Paul's distillation of masculinity, my own, if it existed at all, was infinitely complex. I wondered if I would ever be able to sort that out, and determined to talk with Claude and Pytor about it when next we met.

Paul and Sarah practiced together a little and then did

the dance. It was enchanting. Sarah and the rest of us applauded Paul who, beaming his pleasure, instantly became the fairy. We insisted they do it again, and again it was wonderful. It was noon. Nothing could follow. They all made their goodbyes and left.

We knelt in the window seat and watched them as they came out from under the arcade, Paul to hurry across the square in the direction of the *bistro*. Claude, Pytor, and Monique squeezed into her tiny open car, Claude driving, Monique on Pytor's lap. He spurted off with a roar.

We discussed our long morning, made love, slept, made love. Sarah got up and started to work at my drafting table. She was doing a sculptured set for *The Tempest*. I got a chair, put it beside her, put my arm around her to hold her right breast, in a way to interfere with her, and said, "Not *that* way!

"Make it *round*.

"You *can't* do that!

"It's much too *big!*

"The angle is all *wrong!*

"It's got no *top*."

At the same time I alternately jiggled her arm, squeezed her breast, kissed her, and tickled her ribs. When she was near hysterics I got up and went for my clothes, saying, "All right. If you don't like me I'll go down and talk to the cook. *She* loves me."

"Why? I'm not jealous or anything. Just green with envy."

"I like her. I like cooking."

"I wish I could."

"It's educational, good for the limbs, pleasing to others, gratifying for one's self."

"But you also like servants a lot."

"Some of my best friends are."

"I wish I could get used to them. I'm a little frightened of them. I have some crazy notion, particularly in restaurants, that they're not people. But of course they are. All the time they are. And I don't feel it. I suppose you feel it because you're used to them."

"Probably."

"I suppose I should take a course, 'A Survey of Domestics and Waiters.'"

"It might help."

"Well, give my love to your cook."

"I will. She will appreciate it, even if she thinks I'm kidding."

I started to go. She said, "Kidding is a game you play, isn't it?"

"Yes."

"Why don't you play it with me?"

"I don't really know. Perhaps it's because I love you so much."

"That's no excuse."

"I feel that we are two octopi, our tentacles so intertwined that there is no room for kidding. Kidding is for simple relationships, in space. I feel that I could, inadvertently, hurt you in the heat of exchange, and vice versa. I'm tender as in 'ouch.' I want to love you, be engrossed with you, not have fun with you. Perish the thought."

She threw back her head. I started to go again. She said, "Don't go. I feel you on the verge of a 'Driveling Idiot' mood. I love them. I don't want to miss one."

"'Dithering.'"

"Excuse me, it won't happen again. I'll also take the advice you gave me just now. Will you give up your cook?"

We kissed, tenderly, for a while. She said, "Do take off your clothes. They make me nervous."

I took them off, sat down on a chair at the table, a few feet away from her. I felt that something was coming, that I might need air around me. Swinging room. She said, "I want to ask you a question, seriously. I want to ask you a serious question."

"Which?"

"Quit it, little cretin."

"About the cook?"

"Yes. You feel really comfortable with her, don't you?"

"Yes."

"And you feel really comfortable with Pytor and Claude, because they come from the same kind of background that you do."

"Yes."

"But you don't feel really comfortable with me, do you?"

"No."

"Come on, why?"

'Because you're so exciting for me. Because I cherish you so much. It keeps me up."

"Would you feel really comfortable with me if you were not in love with me?"

"Probably."

"Oh come on. Give."

"Because you're an artist."

"I am. Isn't that surprising. I had never thought of it that way. You are too, it dawns on me, at last."

Pause. She went on, "So you're comfortable with the gentry, and servants, and artists. What about all the myriad rest of mankind?"

"I'm neither comfortable nor uncomfortable with them. Just strange. I don't know them. Just students."

"Are you a snob?"

"I don't know."

"Nevertheless I don't think you would be really comfortable with me even if you were not in love with me. But I love you just the same. I don't really want you comfortable with me. This way we commune."

Her remarks made me profoundly uncomfortable. I put on my clothes and went down to the basement. Is love, after all, simply two people being uncomfortable together in an exciting way? I hoped not. I wanted a mystical union with Sarah.

In the steamy, aromatic kitchen the cook said, "Ah, you're just in time. That eccentric in room fifty-two wants an *Omelette Gratinée aux Champignons,* a salad, bread, and a bottle of *Chablis.* For two. Exquisite, yes? Will you make the omelet? Who is he, anyway? Start with the cream sauce."

"He's an American newspaper man, and not one of my favorite types."

"What have you got against him? The mushrooms are over there."

"He complained about me."

"Why? What did you do?"

"What pan shall I use?"

"That one."

"His room is under mine. Mademoiselle and I were wrestling. We fell off the bed together. It did make quite a thump, but nothing to make all that fuss about. You would have thought his life had been ruined."

"A voyeur, at bottom, no doubt. You should toss her about, Apache style, but then he'd never leave."

"I thought of that. She sends you her love. I'll make him a leather omelet."

"She's after my heart too?"

"Yes."

"Does she know it's of stone?"

"But naturally, what else?"

"But she gave you no handkerchief to bring with you?"

"No."

"Then she doesn't love me. You're safe. You'd better turn on the broiler."

"But I'm not safe. I'm in danger."

"How's that?"

I wasn't quite sure, so I didn't say anything. We worked in silence. After a while I realized I wanted to hear my voice proclaim my love. I said, to the high ceiling, "I *love* Sarah."

The reverberations were good. I smashed the three eggs into the bowl and started to beat them with a fork. I did love her, comfortable or not.

"Your cock's as big as your right arm."

"That's not the half of it."

"Don't boast. But I know what you mean."

"Do you think I have nympholepsy?"

"You certainly show some signs of it today."

"I want union."

"The two are incompatible, you know."

"If I had union, would I know it?"

"Not necessarily. You might only discover it after it was gone."

"Shit. Why does it have to be so complicated?"

I shook the omelet pan, violently.

"You want a rule guaranteed to produce perfect love?"

"Yes. You have to learn how to be a cook, or an architect. Why not?"

"You select a fine frenzy, season it well with an obsession for the unobtainable, cook it in a hot carnal oven, and smother it with affectionate concern. That's the recipe."

"I want our souls in a nimbus, in a *blancmange*."

"*And* a cock as big as your arm."

"Yes. It's as simple as that."

"My poor boy," she said, with feeling. "That omelet must be ready now."

I went back to my room. Sarah was lying the wrong way on the bed, her head propped up on pillows. She had tied a sketchbook to the headboard, had a pencil between the big and second toes of one foot, an eraser between the toes of the other, and was drawing a cat, too concentrated to look at me. I watched her. She writhed, voluptuously.

"Try it."

I took off my clothes and set myself up as she had. It was frustrating but produced fascinating unintended distortions. We tried holding hands. It didn't help. We linked our right hands and our left hands. That seemed to inhibit our hand reactions and release our feet, but it soon got very sexy. We gave up drawing. Later she said, "Let's go out to dinner, to a place where we can see a lot of people walking by, and play Instant Biographies. I feel like hearing your 'exagminations and factifications' about people in progress, tonight. Mine too. And let's stop in at The Standup on the way back. You know why people use it? Because it's practical. The steps allow a tall man and a short woman to fit. That's our problem. Let's try them."

On the way back it was empty and, as always, permeated by the smell of the milk goats' stable. She tried to push me in. I pulled her by it. On the way down to the square she simultaneously rubbed my arm with her breast, banged my fly with her sketchbook, and hit my shoulder with her head.

14

Dear Sarah,

I have not heard from you in some time. I called at your hotel Tuesday. They told me that you were at another hotel around the corner with a young man and that they couldn't know when you would be back and that it was all right for me to call on you there. But I thought better of it because I thought I might be "interrupting." Phillippe and I would like to meet the young man. Can you come to dinner a week from today Thursday eight o'clock just the four of us.

L. Josephine. (Formal)

I found it very funny.

"At last, at last, I'm going to meet your sister."

"Don't be too sure of that, little cretin."

Later she said, "You really do want to meet my sister, don't you?"

"Yes, I really do."

"Why?"

"Even my worst enemies don't call me 'incurious.' "

"All right, I'll take you. You'll have to dress."

"I know, but I'll survive somehow."

"You know, she's really, *really* pretty, not too bright, and voraciously curious about men. Phillippe is exclusively concerned with money and guns. You won't be pleased."

"Just let me meet them. If the rest is dross, I'll still feel amply compensated."

The next Thursday she went to her room to dress. We

arranged to meet in front of my hotel, then take the taxi. I waited in the arcade. It was very cold. She arrived in a Russian fur hat, cocked on her head, a fur coat, a tiny fur muff, and boots. I had not seen that costume, and was overcome. She looked utterly enchanting. We started off for the taxi. When I could stop looking at her I noticed it was not there. We stopped in the middle of the square, on the tree island. I stood off from her, saying, "Model it for me. You're too ravishing. I have to have time to take you in."

She jumped up on The Coffin, modeled it, then caricatured a model, then danced, a sexy, slightly inebriated wood nymph in fur, flinging herself in self-absorbed abandon. People going by laughed and clapped. The taxi came back and stopped next to us, the driver looking at her with grave concern. I opened the door, she jumped down and got in. He said, "Mademoiselle Sarah is ecstatic tonight. Perhaps there is some good news we would all be interested to hear about?"

"No. We're just going to my sister's for dinner."

"Ah, now I understand. Mademoiselle is letting off steam before the semi-catastrophe."

"Yes."

"It's the same with me. I have a brother, you understand. We go to dinner there once a year. He comes to us once a year. Our wives don't get along as well as they might. We drink too much. We have a hangover the next day. That makes the affair worse, the aftermath you understand. My advice is don't drink too much, only a bottle of wine, to be sociable. Where does your sister live?"

She told him. He shut the glass and turned around. We started off. She parted my overcoat, unbuttoned my fly, pulled out my penis, took a small white, lace-edged handkerchief from her muff, wrapped it around the tip, put her muff over it, her hand in the other end and stroked my glans. After a minute it felt marvelous, then more and more so. She watched my face, intently. I came.

"Can you come again?"

"Yes."

After that she took off the muff, rolled down the window a little, and threw the handkerchief out. She said, "I have lots of these. My sister gave them to me," giving me a mysterious, myopic, sexy look.

The house was in a neighborhood remote from city life. Nothing around except other houses. It had a high stone wall around it, with broken glass embedded in the top. There was a huge, bolt-studded wood gate, a small knocker, and a bell button. The taxi driver said, "You'll never get a taxi here at night. Do you want me to come back for you?"

"Yes."

"What time?"

"What's the earliest time we can leave?" I asked Sarah.

"I don't know. You decide."

"Ten-thirty," I told him.

"I'll ring when I get here."

I rang, there was a buzzing sound, and I pushed open the forbidding gate. We walked through a garden to a brightly lit, ornate door, open, with a butler standing in it. He took our coats. We walked in to a large living room, done in decorator-tasteful, comfortable, curiously American in feeling though everything in it was French. There were hunting prints on the walls, mirrors over the two fireplaces, two crystal chandeliers, and a bar in one corner, a tray on a high stand laden with bottles, glasses, tools, an ice bucket and a silver shaker. Sarah walked around the walls looking at the prints, her face a few inches away from them, as if she were half blind, scanning them, inch by inch. I stood in the middle taking deep breaths, got dizzy, sat down on a sofa and looked at the ceiling. Josephine appeared. Her perfume walloped me.

"Oh, here you are. Where's Sarah? Gone to the powder room?"

"I think she's behind that door."

I nodded to the only place I thought she could be.

"Sarah, come out of there and introduce your young man to me."

Sarah emerged from behind the door, looking too composed, and introduced us. Her sister said, while rather obviously sizing me up, "Phillippe was late again getting home from the office. He always is. He's dressing now, and will be down in a little while. In the meantime will you do the honors? I think everything you will need is over there. Sarah, what would you like? I think I would like a dry Martini with a twist of lemon. Sarah, what would you like?"

"A *Vichy*, with ice."

"That's not very exciting, but then, you never have been able to drink. I suppose if you can't it's better to stay away from alcohol altogether. Still, you miss a lot of fun that way. Phillippe has an enormous capacity for alcohol but he seldom has time to drink except when he's shooting. . . ."

I went to the bar and slowly made drinks, while listening to Josephine go on about Phillippe, his life and his times. She was obviously an expert on the subject and, I guessed, a husband-helper, if not a husband-manager.

To see Sarah and Josephine together was an astonishing experience. Beautiful women can complement each other, as showgirls are chosen to do, or inform on the nature of each other's beauty, as the chorus line in a burlesque is chosen. Sarah and my mother were complementary. It was an uncomplicated pleasure to watch them together. Sarah and Josephine informed on each other, forcing me to reassess Sarah, my love, whom I thought I knew so well. I now saw her as a creature based on a hard, handsome bony structure, with a hard layer of muscles attached, covered by a layer of subcutaneous fat which was, miraculously, exactly the right thickness over each part of her body, thickest over her upper arms, stomach and inner thighs, thinnest over her wrists, ankles and eye sockets. Her curves were subdued and flowed into each other. She was all of a piece. Josephine's beauty was of pure flesh, firm, abruptly curved, in high relief. I had always thought Sarah sexy-looking. In contrast with Josephine she looked like a young Greek goddess, an Artemis. I supposed that if I met Josephine on the street, without Sarah, she would seem less voluptuous, that her underlying structure would be more apparent when not in contrast with a beauty I now saw as absolutely pure. It made Josephine seem attractively repellent. I wondered if she realized that.

Phillippe came in, tall, handsome, very well dressed, somehow conveying a lack of self-assurance.

"Have you all got drinks?" he said, looking at them.

"Yes," we all said.

He came to me, shook hands French style, and said, American style, "My name's Phillippe, since no one's going to introduce us. What's yours?"

Josephine said, "Oh darling. Do forgive me. It's so rude to let people hang."

"It's all right, my dear. I learned to overcome small social embarrassments long ago."

I didn't believe him. He went to the bar for a drink. No one told him my name. He did not ask again.

Josephine asked me: "How old are you?"

"Where do you live?"

"Why do you live there?"

"What school do you go to?"

"Do you like it?"

"Do you have friends in Paris?"

"Who do you go around with?"

"He's in the nobility, isn't he?"

"What do you study to become an architect?"

"What does your father do?"

I fell back on my Nice Kid act in which, with infinite politeness, one proffers a minimum of informaton in a maximum of words. Dinner was announced. Josephine took my arm, engulfing me in her heavy perfume, and led me across the front hall to the dining room. It was marble floored, relatively empty of furniture, candle-lit, and very reverberant. Our voices suddenly became overwhelming, our words echoed in crazy space, like richocheting bullets. Sarah fell into one of her Sleeping Beauty moods. Phillippe listened silently, apparently enraptured by it all. Beauty, Nice Kid, clever Josephine, lucky him.

"It's all so romantic," Josephine commented at last, apparently, for the moment, satiated.

"Hardly," I said, "it's really very humdrum."

"But it is! Young love in Paris, carefree student life, wonderful schools, architecture, the stage. Phillippe has told me all about his schools. I envy you three."

"In a romance, something has to happen. There has to be a hero, great and mysterious events, ideals and extraordinary talents."

"Why do you think *The Sun Also Rises* is so romatic then?" Sarah asked me. "The hero has no talents and no ideals. Neither has the heroine. And there are no events worthy of note, really."

"Sarah! You've got it! It's the inside out of a classical romance. A lost instead of a found. The extremes, zero and infinity, feel the same. The means do too. The great well-trodden middle ground. It makes perfect sense."

I wondered what Lady Sybil would think of the notion.

"What are you talking about?" Josephine asked. At the same time Phillippe said, "I am sure you can't apply ratio to life."

"We're talking about art."

"Or to art either. I've never heard it done."

"It's done all the time. My *Patron* spends endless hours comparing detailed mathematical analyses of disparate art objects, including music. He asked a friend of mine, who worked for him, into his living room to hear him play the Venus de Milo on the piano."

I did not add that Pytor had said it was farcical.

"I was not thinking of art," Josephine said. "I was thinking of real life. Love, particularly young, carefree love, is romantic. Aren't you romancing Sarah?"

"No. I'm not romancing little old Sarah."

Josephine's laugh reverberated.

"And you, Sarah, aren't you romancing him?"

"I'm afraid not. But it might be a good idea."

She gave me a flirtatious smile, just short of an out-and-out parody of what she did naturally. I said, "I think of a

truly romantic tale as that of Orpheus and Eurydice, and so
did Gluck, obviously."

Josephine said, "I can't remember what they all did."

I had had enough, so I told them, in minute and fulsome
detail, worried by the power of my voice in that strange
room. After a while I began to realize that I was working
myself up, which made me mad, and worse, behaving
exactly as my mother would. "He was so boring I decided
to tell him the story of my life," she said of someone. I
got Eurydice back in Hades and Orpheus on his wander-
ings in a hurry, turned to Phillippe, and asked him what
kind of shotgun he preferred. He told me, in minute detail.
He's getting even with me, I thought, but likably.

The taxi was announced at last. We said our goodbyes
and got in. Sarah asked, "What happened?"

"I don't know."

"I don't remember anything from the time you went
into your Nice Kid act, except the part about *The Sun
Also Rises.*"

"Didn't you go into your Sleeping Beauty act?"

"Yes. I suppose I did. I suppose that's why I can't remember. Or do you think I'm crazy?"

"No. We were doing the same thing, according to our
separate abilities and talents, which, combined, are without
number."

Sarah, I was glad to see, away from Josephine, had re-
gained her sexy look, was less the goddess, more the
nymph. I put my arm around her, my other hand in her
muff, and held hers inside it.

"You had a great idea," I said.

"It wasn't an idea. It was an observation. You had the
idea. You live in your head a lot. I live in my underpants.

Come to think of it, maybe I should start wearing them. A home away from home."

"Oh no, please don't. I like the thought of you nice and round and cleft down there between your legs, naked."

"Will you, some day, just grab me there, under my skirt?"

"Yes, my love."

"And will you, some day, give me some flowers?" she said, giving me the most heart-rending, longing look.

"Yes. A nosegay. In memoriam of some advice you once gave me, about noses and vulvas, if I don't die of my love for you first."

We rubbed noses. She said, "I worry that I can't defend myself."

"Why do you have to?"

"You always have a reason for everything."

"There are both verbal and graphic ideas, you know. Artists really shouldn't talk. They do it badly. They should leave the talking to verbal types, and get on with their art, whatever it is."

"Where does that leave you, little cretin?"

"I'm a Pushmepullyou, you're a deer."

"Nevertheless, I wish I could have a clear-cut idea, and then carry it out."

"I'm coming to the conclusion that nobody does. You just have to muck around until something happens."

The taxi driver slid back the glass behind him and asked, "Where do you want to go?"

"Your stand. We'll go to the *bistro*, to cool Mademoiselle off."

"You're a jockey, then."

"But yes."

"I'll come in and sit with you, if you don't mind. I want to hear about your evening."

We took a table. I described the evening for him.

"I understand," he said. "It's typically bourgeois."

He got up and held out his palm. I reached for my wallet. I'd forgotten it. I looked the question at Sarah. She shook her head.

"We both forgot our money. I'll go over and get some for you. Be right back."

"Don't bother. Give it to me in the morning. But don't forget. After all, money is money. You can't live on romance, you know."

"True, but you can dine out on it."

"What if I had been a strange taxi driver?"

"I would have been terribly embarrassed."

"There you are. You would have had to borrow from Mademoiselle's sister or brother-in-law. Broke is the wrong way to approach the bourgeois. It would not have been very romantic."

"It wasn't anyway."

"Romance is for the aristocracy. The rest of us just struggle."

"You're a knight of the pavements, in any case."

"I am, you know."

He went to the bar and paid for us. I said, "I gave him the wrong impression. It was really *bogus* bourgeois. I can't tell how Phillippe conveys his lack of assurance, or how Josephine conveys her greediness, or how the house conveys their air of not really belonging to anything."

"Would you like to give my sister a fast poke?"

"In theory, yes. In practice I don't think I could."

"How did you like my diddling kit?"

"It was liberating. I loved it. In fact I simply adored it. You're an angel."

"I wanted you to arrive with your knockers empty. I thought it might help. Did it?"

"If you mean did it affect my reactions to your sister, I think not. That sort of thing is in the mind. That's why I don't think I could poke her. My psyche would surely turn off my animal, so there's no point in even thinking about it."

"That's good to know. If you thought you could, I'd scratch her eyes out."

"Why her eyes, not mine?"

"Because I value yours too much, my love, in sickness and in health, in knockers and in psyche."

We left. It was then bitterly cold. We blew vapor clouds at each other as we crossed the square.

15

My dissatisfaction with Old Stroph, and my sense of the school as a whole as stationary, as mired in its conservative traditions, become intolerable. It was impossible to really talk to Old Stroph in the *Atelier*. I called up his wife and made an appointment to see him in his apartment-office. When I got there she answered the door. She was a favorite of mine, an enchanting old lady, shriveled up and warped by arthritis, amusing and outgoing.

"Ah, it's you," she said.

"Who else? How are you?"

"Fine. But is it really you?"

"I don't know. I've been thinking about that as I walked here."

The entrance hall behind her was lined with books, from floor to ceiling.

"Do I sense an air of rebellion?"

"You do, I'm afraid."

"Courage. He expects you. Don't talk to him about architectural books, particularly new ones from England and America. I can't stand another book in this house. I'm going crazy. Promise?"

"Promise."

"I'll have to trust you. I'll knock."

Old Stroph, from inside the door bellowed, "Enter!"

I felt scared. As I opened the door she put a finger over her lips, hunkered down even more than she did naturally, and backed away, a conspirator. The door was not yet shut when he said, "Have you received any new books from England or America?"

"No. I'm afraid not."

"But you do get the English and American magazines?"

"Yes."

"Do you save them?"

"Yes."

"How many do you have?"

"A lot. I don't know how many exactly."

"Will you do something for me?"

"Of course."

"Go through them all and pick out the things you think uniquely English or American. Put a bookmark in, and write a *précis* of why you think so. Then give them to me. I won't promise to give them all back."

"I'd love to!" I was thrilled.

"I might do something for you sometime. But it's unlikely. So what?"

"I came to ask a favor."

"I knew that."

"I want to do contemporary architecture, really contemporary."

"You mean stuff such as that fellow, what's his name, Le Courvoisier does?"

"Le Corbusier and Pierre Jeanneret. Yes."

"But why, in God's name? It's ugly. Just flat planes with holes banged in them. No chiaroscuro. No soul."

"They're functional."

"They're sure to fall apart in no time. What's functional about that?"

"They're full of light, and in the new materials, glass, concrete, steel."

"Such materials are not new. They're used in all buildings. Those chaps, the Germans, are faddists, like the Cubists."

"They use materials in a way appropriate to their nature. Glass in large sheets the way it's manufactured, not cut up for style's sake. Concrete in flat planes because of form work. Flat roofs because you don't need all that structure and tile."

"Do you really feel that way? Do you want to destroy the great classic tradition?"

"I don't know. I was brought up in it. I want to find out whether I can feel in this new way. I want something *real* to do. I want to think of *real* people in buildings, doing *real* things."

"My poor boy. You realize that you will fail design if you take such a stand. I could not defend you against my colleagues, even if I really wanted to. I think you have talent. But that sort of thing is childish. It's outlandish."

"Then I'm going to have to give up school."

"Wait. Let's not be hasty. I can see you're really serious."

"I am."

"Would you mind losing credit for one problem?"

"No."

He rummaged around in his desk drawer and came up with a mimeographed program.

"This is the program you are about to get. It's a small theatre for Louis XIV. Go through it and black out all references to Louis XIV. Design it as you would if a client came to you with the commission today. Don't go to the

Atelier at all. This has to be a private matter, strictly between us. Bring it here on the due date. Good day."

"Thank you very much," I said, sincerely grateful, tremendously relieved, even though I knew he was setting a trap for me. He wanted to make me compare a rank experiment with a well understood and documented formula.

In the hall, his wife appeared. She whispered, "How did it go?"

"Well."

"Books?"

"I avoided that, but I couldn't avoid magazines."

"Heaven help us. He's so unpredictable."

"Thank heaven!"

I went to the nearest café, ordered coffee, read the program several times, borrowed the café pen and cut the idiot thing, in successive operations, to a skeleton. On the way to Sarah's I stopped at the Post Office and mailed it to him. I knew it by heart. If he wanted me now, he'd have to find me. Sarah said, "You've been so long! What happened with Old Stroph?"

I told her.

"I have a feeling that you're in for trouble. Will you leave if the experiment turns out badly?"

"Yes."

"Then what?"

"I don't know."

"You worry me."

"Will you help me?"

"I don't think I can. I know a lot about how to use a theatre that's already there, but I seldom think about a theatre in the abstract. The idea is foreign to me. It's architectural. But I'll compromise. I'll sit in your lap with your cock in me if you so wish, while you work over my shoulder. I'll read Balzac over yours. O. K.?"

"A splendid scheme."

"How are you going to find out about theaters in this morass?"

I thought about that, furiously.

"Oh dear! I'm going to lose you, my love, am I not?"

"Yes, but only temporarily."

We made love and went out to lunch. After lunch I went to the one magazine in France which published contemporary architecture. The front office looked like an upper-class English pub. I went through the index, looked up a few things, found nothing of any real interest. Through, I went to the bar and asked the secretary behind it if I could see an editor. I blushed.

"Why?"

"I would like to ask for a job."

"Here?"

"Yes."

"Are you some kind of an eccentric?"

"No. I'm an architectural student."

"My poor boy. I'll get him."

She came back with an utterly disreputable type whom I recognized as one of the really old and seldom seen members of Old Stroph's studio. He looked as if he had slept in his clothes, his tie was undone, his cuffs were hiked up just a little, French fashion. I judged him thirty-five. He put his elbows on the bar and said, very rapidly, "Come, come. What do you want? Speak up! I don't have all day, you know. Speak up! Speak up! Why do you just stand there. Good God, are you a deaf mute? *Please* tell me what you want. Quickly, if you don't mind. Who *are* you? I can't hear you. Are you sick? Constipated perhaps? No, don't say a word."

I collapsed into helpless laughter. He put his hands over his face.

"You're the poor boy with the beautiful American girl. All right, what is it?"

"I am an architectural student. I speak English."

"I know that. *For God's sake what do you want?*"

"A part-time job making *précis* of interesting things from the English language magazines."

"It might be an idea. Bring me three samples. Then we'll talk about money, but we won't talk much about it. Understand?"

"Yes."

When I told Sarah about it she said, "You *are* a coony type. What are you going to do with the money if you get the job?"

"Take you to Venice."

I got the job and much later we went to Venice, but that is too sensuous a story to recount, involving a tempest, a large marble bathtub in which we fed each other with our hands, while penetrating each other in various ways, and read Dickens out loud to each other, curled up, naked, in a great armchair.

The theatre was a tremendous strain. There was very little basic information later than nineteen hundred, no published contemporary examples not based on traditional ideas, one German project, Walter Gropius' "Total Theater," the plans for which were more or less un-understandable to me. Sarah's detailed information was upsetting, more specific than I could manage before having reached a basic concept. I used up roll after roll of sketch paper, the floor was covered with discarded trials. I flew into rages and shouted obscenities at my drawings. Then Sarah would sit on my lap and nibble me avidly. It was impossible not to pay attention to that, but my difficulties, particularly those with aesthetics, oppressed me every second of every day and night. I felt in a strait-jacket.

I worked through the night of the day before it was due. That morning I looked up to see Sarah, lying on my bed on her stomach, propped up on her elbows, her knees drawn to her sides, flat on the bed, her forelegs against her thighs. She was reading. Her bottom was aimed directly at me, her vulva was open, her anus fully exposed, pink, in a little cup of flesh. I had never, that I could remember, seen an anus. Her odd, almost unbelievably flexible pose, and the view it afforded of her crotch was overpowering. I sprang erect, jumped up, sprang on her body, put two fingers in her, pummeling her with my other hand, then punched, scratched, and hit her. She made sounds of surprise, of reaction, but not of displeasure. I didn't want that, got much rougher, and finally pinched both her stretched labia between the nails of thumb and index fingers, hard. She cried out and struggled. We fell off the bed, hitting the floor together with a tremendous thud. I twirled her around, pressed back her legs, locked her up, squeezed her mightily, coupled, and banged her as hard and as fast as I could. I thudded on her. She thudded on the floor, whimpering continuously. I breathed hard. It was noisy, rough, and long drawn out. I finally came explosively, my last spurt of semen immediately followed by an awful sense of remorse.

"How could I?"

"It's all right."

"I love you. I don't want to rape you, hurt you."

"I know. It's all right, really it is. You're just a bit edgy. I'll recover."

"Oh Sarah!" in despair.

"Let me go, my love. You're squeezing me to death."

"Sarah!"

"It's my fault. Now don't think about it any more and go back to work. I don't want you to get really mad at me."

I went back to my drafting board surprised and dismayed at myself. Had she tempted me on purpose to see what kind of a reaction she would get? I thought that perhaps she had, felt better then, and went back to work.

After lunch, eaten silently while I worked, Sarah said, "I want to go do some errands. I'll be back when you see me."

She came back in the middle of the afternoon.

"I called my sister, among other things. She has a letter from my mother and wants to talk about it. I asked her to tea. You don't have to pay any attention. You're in the clouds anyway. I hope you don't mind."

"Not at all."

"I ordered tea from your waiter on the way up. A big tea. He said that you should get some exercise, not draw all the time, go for a walk. I told him you were getting plenty, in your own way."

"You *are* mad at me."

"No, my love, I'm not."

She kissed me all over my face, then asked, "Do you want me to nigger for you?"

"Yes, my love, I do."

We flattened the board so that she could work opposite me, and I put her to drawing theatre seats. Before five she put on one of my favorite dresses, white, a cone bisected, low towards the back, tiny straps, so simple that she shone forth. Very high heels. Josephine arrived, filling the room with her pervasive perfume, followed by my waiter with the tray. He gave her the same rapt attention he had given Monique, but for biological rather than social reasons. Sarah turned into a goddess again. The two sisters stood facing each other, Sarah's legs wide apart in a stance she sometimes took, stunning. She described for Josephine our morning's encounter. No detail was left out. At the end she swept off her dress. Her mons was blue, red, and purple. My fingernail marks showed. I felt horrified at myself for doing it, and expected Josephine to castigate me. Instead she said, "That's wonderful. I wondered about him. I wish my Phillippe would act that way occasionally. He's wonderful, but he doesn't go at me that way. There's very little excitement. Still, I love him. I know he cheats occasionally. That's his way. But I also know he will never have a mistress, not even me. That's reassuring for the long run."

Sarah said, "My love has never seen anybody's vulva but mine. Will you let me show him yours?"

"Yes. I'd like to."

She took off her dress. She had on a pink lace brassiere and pink lace panties. She took them off and sat down on the foot of the bed. Her breasts were fleshy and pendulous in a wonderful way, the aureola small, dark, and prominent. Her pubic hair was thick, curly, and luxuriant. I wondered why I had never questioned the fact that Sarah had none. Sarah got a drafting pencil and sat down beside her.

"Come," she said to me, "get a chair so you can see."

Josephine lay back and spread her legs, one in Sarah's lap. Sarah, rubbing each part with the round end of the pencil said, "You see, lots of pubic hair. I have none. I had very little to begin with and I pulled it out until it didn't grow any more. Pubic bone. Labia majora, not as big as mine. That's why her nymphae project so prominently. Of course they are much bigger than mine too. This place, between her anus and the bottom of the labia majora is called the perineum. That fold of skin is the fourchet. Anus."

She put the tip of the pencil in.

"Open," she commanded her sister. Josephine spread her labia with both hands. Sarah went on, rubbing the parts with the pencil.

"This is the prepuce, the hood over her clitoris. You see it's much bigger than mine. This is the meatus, the pee-hole. You can't see mine at all. And this is the introitus, much bigger than mine because she has had babies. So you see I'm quite different. She is more or less average. I am underdeveloped except for my labia majora. I have all these parts, of course, but they just didn't expand to this extent. I'll show you later. Now watch here. You'll see the clitoris come down out of its hood."

She diddled the hood lightly and rapidly with the flat of the pencil. The clitoris appeared below it, then abruptly disappeared. Josephine's stomach swelled huge, creased, she clutched her breasts with both hands, her face contorted, then smoothed away to the virginal radiance I had so often seen in Sarah. She opened her eyes and smiled at me.

"Did you like that?" she asked.

"Yes, very much. It was beautiful. Thank you so much."

"Good. I've always wanted to do something like that, for someone like you."

She moved back to the head of the bed and sat up, leaning against the pillows, her legs crossed.

"I suppose Sarah has told you about me. You might think I would have run into an opportunity like this, but I never did. I never met anybody like you or like Sarah. I suppose that you two are the kind of people who find each other even though you're different. But you don't have security. I think you're both too intense. I suppose that's why you love each other that way. It's very noticeable— did you know that? Phillippe says the two of you are 'a phenomenon.' It stands out. But you could kill each other that way, you know. Had you thought about that? You're interesting people. I never thought about you that way, Sarah. Isn't it funny when it's so obvious? Now you're not only more beautiful but more interesting than I am. I should have helped you in those days, but you wouldn't let me and I didn't know how. I suppose you both think Phillippe and I are dull. I'll have to talk to him about that. But you should settle down. Phillippe and I found each other. We're not like you two but we have security. We're both satisfied with that. You should think about it."

She stopped, obviously wanting to say more, agonizingly unable to frame her thought. I guessed that it was something like "Companionate Marriage," did not want to discuss it, and handed her her cup of tea, while Sarah, apparently of the same mind, said, "Do tell me about mother. You worried me on the phone this afternoon."

"The letter is in my bag."

I went back to my drafting board. Sarah got up, found the letter, read it, got her tea, and sat cross-legged, erect, on the foot of the bed facing her sister, her back to me, lithe, handsome, lovely bun low on her neck. They started a long discussion of what to do about their mother's future. I tuned it out, but looked at them often and wondered about Josephine's strange, heavy perfume. They were enchanting. I thought again of my bed alcove's power, with its low ceiling, low lighting, intimate theatrical quality, to make people look their best. And I thought of the feelings I had had, the first time I had met Josephine, about the galvanizing effect their separate styles of beauty had on each other, more marked now that I could compare them nude and relaxed. They held their teacups in the same way, out from their bodies. As dusk fell their skin glowed pink. I wanted them there, in those poses, forever.

But Josephine got up, finally, and started to dress, saying, "I must go home now. I want to be there before Phillippe. When he gets home he likes to have a drink and tell me about his day, and I like to hear about it. That's our best time together. You two can't do that because you're together all the time. What do you talk about? Why don't you have one place, with a bathroom? Then you could get to know each other. It wouldn't cost you any more. I wish you would explain to me sometime what you're doing. Oh I know you're both going to school and all that, but what are you *really* doing. I *must* go. Come and see us soon."

I worked through the night, my second. Fatigue increased my dissatisfactions with my theatre, abated my satisfactions. At two I reached a nadir. Sarah had long since been asleep. I looked out the window for a while, at the empty square, the twinkling gas lights, the black *bistro*, the abandoned taxi, then got Sarah's sketchbook, drew two intertwined red hearts in it, and wrote across them in purple ink:

> *Sarah my dearly beloved one i want you part of me and*
> *i long to be part of you so shall we consume each other*

tender and tasty starting with our big toes ending with our mouths which will meld and smile in bliss then our waiters will put our smile on a branch of the tree in the square and it will radiate our love and they will say that is the best thing that has happened to french aboriculture ever Sarah my dearly beloved my darling?

My first love letter. I propped the sketchbook up on a chair near the foot of the bed so she would see it when she got up. At seven I cut my stretch, rolled it up, and wrote Sarah a note:

This place is too full of my woes. Let's meet in your room.

I put that under the other and went out to breakfast, bleary-eyed.

There was a crisis of some sort going on at Old Stroph's, people tiptoeing about, doors shutting in the inner depths, telephones ringing. His wife did not appear. I waited interminably. Finally he opened his door. We shook hands.

"Put it on my desk."

I did, found some weights, and flattened it. He took one look at it and said, "A catastrophe, no?"

"Yes."

"My poor boy! Now will you take my advice?"

"No."

"Tell me what you found out? I can see not much, but you must have discovered one tiny little something."

I told him at some length. He seemed interested.

"My wife is an acquaintance of your mother's."

"I know, that's where I first met her."

"Had you thought of going to America, to Harvard or Yale or M. I. T.? You're a half thawed-out type. Maybe

M. I. T. would suit you for now. Do you want to try it?"
"Not really, right now. I'd like to stay here." I blushed.
He looked at me quizzically.
"A little friend?"
"Yes, but that's not all. It's more complicated."
"Hm," and then he roared, making me jump, "I adore
my wife!"
"She *is* wonderful."
"Why don't you go see Professor Piatagorsky? You
know Pytor."
I was stunned. It was obviously the perfect solution.
Why hadn't I thought of it? But I had.
"Do you want me to call him?" he asked.
"Yes, if you would be so kind."
He did, and gave Professor Piatagorsky a description of
me so glowing I did not recognize myself. I spoke to him
briefly, overcome with the enormity and rapidity of it all,
thanked Old Stroph from the bottom of my heart, and left.
I felt profoundly exhilarated. On the way to Sarah's I
stopped at the *bistro* and ordered coffee and aquavit. I had
never had it before, nor a drink in the morning. I took
them out to the terrace. My waiter came over for his mid-
morning glass of wine. We said good morning and shook
hands. He got his wine, came back out, and sat down with
me, saying, "Would you mind explaining to me what happened?
I did. He said, "You really worried me with that glass.
I suspected a disaster, you understand. Instead it's a triumph
for French education. Mademoiselle has gone to her hotel.
Why don't you go there and tell her about it. I'll clean up
your room. Have an adequate lunch."
After I told Sarah she put her arms around me and clung,

her head on my chest, saying, "I've been terrified for a whole month. I thought that if it didn't work out you would want to go somewhere else, and that we would have to part. I couldn't bear the thought. I need you more than you know. Now we can have a whole other year together."

We made love and went out to lunch. I said, "Your anatomy lesson gave me a set of ideas. I want to experiment, examine you all over, measure you, see the inside of your vagina. Would you mind?"

"No. I'd welcome it because I feel the same way about you. I'd like to know you, clinically. It sounds rather gruesome, and I don't mean we should ever stop making love. But I do want to try out all sorts of things."

"How do you see a vagina?"

"With a speculum."

"Can we get one?"

"Yes. And I want to get a magnifying glass, to see your skin and hair, some sculptor's calipers, and two dildoes, to fill our holes. Can we get them at No. 5?"

"I don't know, but they surely could tell us where we can buy them, if they don't sell them themselves."

We went shopping.

16

One Sunday we were finishing a group of drawings Sarah had done ex school. They were all over the floor and looked marvelous, warm, fresh, full of ideas. Among them were also some drawings we had done together, of ourselves, inspired by Leonardo da Vinci's illustration for "The Golden Rule." We had measured each other for them, and had overlaid them with geometrical figures designed to show the relationship of various points of the body—crotch, navel, nipples, chin—to the whole. Discarded trials, crumpled up, were everywhere. Every available surface was covered with paints, pastels, tools of all sorts, brushes in jars, paper, a myriad of things. Our faces and bodies were splattered with paint and grimy with graphite. The room smelled deliciously of our supplies. We were intent, and very happy. Sarah had her hair in braids with ribbons, which I liked for aesthetic, sexual, and playful reasons. They made her look infantile. There was a knock on the door. I called, "Who is it?"

"Nelson. Let me in."

"Bad Clutch," I called, cordially, "just a second."

I whipped on a Chinese robe and skullcap I kept for such occasions. It did not look like a bathrobe, and threw people off. Sarah whipped on a smock. I opened the door. He stepped in and leaned against the jamb, cocky, ebullient, impeccably dressed, the very image of upper-class Golden Youth. I introduced him to Sarah.

"What brings you here?" I asked. I had heard that he was going to Harvard.

"I've been going around the world with my mother, as usual."

"Where did you go?"

"San Francisco, Tokyo, Hong Kong, Peking, that way around. I really can't remember many details. Mother saw friends and went to museums. Just now she was talking to your mother on the phone, asking her to dinner. I scuttled off, before she could think of asking us. Well, let's see. I got mildly sloshed at lunch, played tennis with pros and pickups in the afternoons. I've really gotten good. I'll beat the shit out of you now, old friend. But where was I? I saw a lot of my old waiter and chambermaid buddies, screwed a few of the latter for old times' sake. I got sloshed at dinner. Then I'd repair to the local riding academy, otherwise known as the whorehouse, and screw my little heart out. Mornings were exclusively devoted to hangovers. I am now an international authority on pigs and pig environments. I'll tell you all about them, intellectually, at dinner tonight. Intellectually because that's the only language you understand, and I'm sure your 'little friend' here must be one too, otherwise she wouldn't be your 'little friend,' and at dinner because the two of you are going to have dinner with me, caviar and champagne, at the Maisonette. Nine o'clock. Give me a drink. I'm done in by this epic review of my life. You always affect me that way and never have any booze a body can wet his whistle with. I should have come prepared. I'm off."

He started to go, then turned around in the doorway.

"Marjory Islington was in Hong Kong with us, and her mother. My mother said, 'She's suitable for you, Nelson.

She will be very well off someday.' I decided to try romance. I figured that a cunt that never had had any would be hotter than Aunt Jemima's Boston Baked Bean Pot. We played tennis and danced. She's good at both, as you know. One night I kissed her. She was like the top of a totem pole. 'Open wide,' I told her. 'This won't hurt a bit.' 'Ah,' she said. I ruffled her boobs to see if that would heat her up a bit. 'Please Nelson,' she said 'don't be vulgar.' I started to laugh, then I lost control of myself and rolled around on the grass. When I came to, she was gone. I met her in the lobby the next day. She said, 'I have decided to forgive you, Nelson.' I started to laugh again. End of romance.

"Oh, and one more bit of news. I read *War and Peace* on the trip, and I want to discuss it with you. You're about the only friend I have who can do that sort of thing. Pity you don't screw too. Then we'd really be buddies. Or have your reformed?"

He gave Sarah a salacious look and left.

"Is that the little boy you described so charmingly, under the trees, who played Puck in *A Midsummer Night's Dream?*"

"The same."

"Was he kidding?"

"No. It's all too true. He's always led that kind of life, trailing his mother from place to place, brought up by hotel chambermaids and waiters, being kicked out of improbable schools for rich delinquents. A waiter took him to his first brothel when he was thirteen. He's had several venereal diseases. He's really a waif. If we go, you will hear more of the same, in more gruesome detail."

"But you accepted!"

"Not really. I didn't say anything. If we don't go it will make no difference. He may not even remember he asked us by nine. Would you like to go?"

"Yes. I'm curious."

"All right, but let's insist on caviar and champagne only. Then we can make a quick getaway if the going gets rough. Bad Clutch likes to get people drunk. You'll have to be firm about the champagne."

The Maisonette was a very good restaurant run by White Russians. It was small, cluttered, shabby, and had a beautiful bar along one wall, separated from the main room by a row of columns. An accordionist walked about playing teary Russian tunes. It had a devoted clientele. When we got there Bad Clutch was standing at the bar, his back against it, surveying the scene morosely. He spied us and began to ogle Sarah with a covert obscene slyness, enough to irritate but not infuriate. We took a table. He ordered a mountain of caviar in a scooped out block of ice, a magnum of extraordinarily dry California champagne for us, vodka for himself. I said, "I heard that you were going to Harvard. What happened? How did you get in?"

"You don't think it was my brains and beauty, do you? You know me too well for that. So it has to be my money and my family."

He said that with real smugness, paused to let it sink in, and went on, "Anyway, I never intended to go to Harvard. I just wanted to visit there. I had to get in to do that. I want to be able to say, whenever I choose, 'Well, when I was at Harvard the . . . ,' or "My Harvard training taught me at least one thing, that . . . ,' or 'As I observed, whilst an undergraduate, the Harvard fraternity of scholars, I came to the conclusion that. . . .' So, appropriate strings were pulled, I moved into the freshman dormitories, spent a month getting the feel of the place, and in dulcet dalliance with the Cambridge whores, who are not in large supply, and as rum a bunch of pigs as I have ever been forced to associate with. If you want a good screw in Boston go to niggertown, I think it's called Roxbury."

Between breaths he gulped whole small glasses of vodka. Sarah and I gorged ourselves on beluga caviar. I drank both my own and Sarah's champagne. Our waiter hovered over us, constantly replenishing. Bad Clutch went on, "When the day for my planned deliverance arrived, I got a black pig and a white pig, took them to my room with plenty of the finest vodka, befuddled them and myself, stripped them and myself, tickled them and goosed them, causing loud whoresome laughter. No one paid any attention. I began to feel desperate. The one thing I can't stand is being ignored. The nigger pig suddenly had to piss. It came to me. I took her to the window and urged an interesting experiment on her, crouched on the window sill. When she was in full flow I grabbed her, so she wouldn't fall out into the Yard, though it was only a short drop, and goosed her, fulsomely. She shrieked, whorishly. I pissed next. Then I urged the same experiment on the white cunt. She screamed girlishly, as I recall. The proctor came and quickly freed me of all care. Harvard became history."

He gulped his vodka.

"But I had gotten a taste for the intellectual life, so I stayed on for a month, in a cheap flophouse, where I could act myself without shame or blame. My mother thought I was still in school. My friends, both high and low, were entranced by my digs, which were known variously by such appelations as The Fuckery, The Boozery, Sodomy Hall . . ."

At that point a very pretty well-dressed girl came up to him, a taut little yacht of a tart.

"Marie-Louise!" he exclaimed, switching to fluent chambermaid French. "My dearest one, my dove. You're late. I've been completely disconsolate, fearing for your safety."

When she got settled, with caviar and champagne, he said, in English, "She's my newest tart. Isn't she unbelievable? I had to show her to you. She's a gem. A little stupid, but then who wants an intelligent tart. What you need is an educated cunt. She's got one."

"In French," Marie-Louise said.

He tossed off a glass and, in French, said, "Marie-Louise was conceived on a cliff in Brittany, in the moonlight. That's why she's so fresh and virginal. The cliff was steep, breakers rolled in to the beach below. The sea was sparkling in the moonlight. The top of the cliff was verdant with long grass, rustling in the gentle balmy breeze. Marie-Louise's mother was in the dog position, looking for insects with a flashlight." (We had done that as children.) "Her father, horny and hairy, crept up behind her mother, aimed his mammoth cock carefully, rammed it home manfully, and came off. Her mother gave a great cry: 'Eureka!' "

Then he sang, in English, imitating Maurice Chevalier, "Every little breeze whispers Mary Louise."

"In French," Marie-Louise said, laughing, sipping champagne.

"Shush. Don't interrupt. You're not conceived yet. The sperm rushed up through her mother's apparatus, looking for the egg. The fastest was the cutest little girl sperm the other sperms had ever seen. She plunged in to the egg and at that precise instant there was a flash of lightning out over the sea and a tremendous thunderclap. Marie-Louise was conceived."

We all laughed. Marie-Louise said, "Oh, my dear, it wasn't that way at all."

"How do you know? You weren't born yet. I haven't gotten to that part of your biography."

"I just know, that's all."

"Shall I go on?"

"No. You'll only embarrass your friends. You're such a kidder."

"But I want to embarrass my friends. That's what they're for."

I knew he meant it. But before he could launch his scheme, whatever it was, two English friends of ours came in. They were as alike as Tweedledum and Tweedledee, inseparable, tweedy, nice, and a little sad. They sat down on either side of the girls.

"Are you two chaps still married?" Bad Clutch asked.

"Well yes, in a way," one said. "That is, we're still together. We still have some time to go, you know."

"Have you considered having children? It could be done, you know. All you need is a big enough cunt for two cocks at a time. I would recommend an ovoid model."

I felt the time had come to go, but before I was up Paul appeared. I introduced him. He kissed Sarah's hand possessively, kissed Marie-Louise's, and shook hands with the rest of us. I could see that we were not his cup of tea at that moment, but said, "Sit down with us, and have some champagne, it's sensational."

"I must fly to the bar to await a friend," he said, and did, comically.

Bad Clutch got up and followed him.

I asked the two English boys, "What are you two doing these days?"

"Writing songs."

"We do it together."

"We both work on both the music and the lyrics."

"Lieder?"

"No. Jazz songs. We hope to get Ambrose to play them."

The accordionist was out at that moment.

"Sing us one."

They did, together, obviously well practiced. It was very good.

"That's nice," Marie-Louise said. "Music is international, I've always heard. Translate the words for me."

They did.

"Why, that's marvelous," Marie-Louise said. "It's so tender and gay."

They beamed.

"Sing us another," I asked. They did. That too was very good. One of them said, "I say, do you suppose Bad Clutch might help us get them played? He knows so many hotel orchestra leaders."

"I have no idea. Why don't you ask him?" I said, feeling despicable. I tossed down a glass of champagne, Bad Clutch fashion. The waiter filled it again, before it was really back on the table.

They started to get up.

"No, wait," I said, my compassion returning. "Don't ask him. When he comes back we'll start our conversation exactly as we did before. I'll ask you what you're doing, ask you to sing, and so on."

I turned to Marie-Louise.

"And you, my dear, say the same things you said before, too."

"No. I can't. I'd get it wrong for sure."

There was a depressing silence, then a muted commotion at the bar. Bad Clutch was standing facing Paul, blood pouring from his mouth. The bar man was signaling someone.

"Stay here," I said to Sarah and Marie-Louise. The two boys and I went slowly to the bar. Bad Clutch was obviously in pain, blood all over his chin and shirt.

"What's the matter?" I asked.

"I was needling this fucking fairy. He reached out and scratched my gums with his fingernails. My mouth was open, naturally."

"Let's take you to a doctor."

The bar man said, "We are calling our regular doctor now. I'll take him to a private room."

The two English boys said, "We'll go with him. You look after the girls."

I frowned at Paul, went back to the table, told them what had happened, and said to Marie-Louise, "We must go. Will you wait for him? I don't think he'll be long."

"I'll wait," she said, "He might need love after such an experience. I enjoyed meeting you, you're a nice boy, I can see that, and you, dear," turning to Sarah, "are beautiful."

Sarah gave her a dazzling smile. I realized that she had said not a word to Bad Clutch, or any of the four other people we had met.

We walked back to Sarah's slowly, she peppering me with questions about the three boys and how they got to be the way they were. Sad stories. As we walked down the rue des Chèvres, I suddenly felt liberated, lucky beyond belief. When we got to the entrance of the milk goats, and The Standup, I pressed her in. We coupled, without moving, as the working class people did. It got agonizing. I willed myself, passionately, to wholly possess her. She made little noises of surprise and apprehension, swelled up, and struggled against my chest. I pressed her harder against the stone embrasure, and came, explosively. She screamed into my shoulder, got rigid, and finally subsided.

"What happened to you?" I asked.

"I got frightened."

"Why?" I asked, incredulous.

"Because I could feel your will in me. I was too penetrated. It was too much you. After you came and I screamed it was stupendous. I do thank you for that, my love, but now that we've done it, we don't have to do it again, unless you wish it."

I 7

Monique and Claude, Sarah and I liked to go dancing in nightclubs. We often went to Bricktops's, a place with a good American Negro band, run by a red-headed American Negro woman, a perfect spot of its kind. It had an international clientele. We were often picked up. Claude and I, in particular, enjoyed the improbable types we met in this way, and the improbable conversations we had with them. If they were bizarre enough, and thoroughly phony, Sarah and I sometimes took them to my mother's, where they blossomed. She pretended, convincingly, to take them at exactly face value.

Pytor joined us on these expeditions infrequently, we thought because he felt a fifth wheel. Then one day he turned up with a mistress. Her name was, confusingly, also Monique. We called her Aussim, liked her very much, but found her an odd choice on Pytor's part. She was pretty enough, with a really splendid figure, wanted to be a dental technician, drank too much, loved practical tricks, in which she often used props, and which were intended to disconcert. She was the daughter of an eccentric druggist in a tiny village in the *Midi*, who kept a cow and invented improbable moving objects, often operated by celestial clocks. She had an apparently limitless fund of marvelously funny stories about her father and village life. I envied her her father and the richness of her life with him.

We were all picked up, on the terrace of the Lutetia, by

an old Arab. After telling us that he was a millionaire and very well thought of in Moroccan circles, he described a bathroom in his mansion, which had six of the most expensive *bidets*, in a row, and asked us if we would all sit on them at once. Afterwards, he said, he would take us to dinner at Foyot's. Aussim said, "That's certainly a very generous offer, but as far as I'm concerned it's impossible. I'm terrified of *bidets*, and I'm deformed because of one."

"But how could that be?" the Arab asked, incredulously.

"When I was fifteen my father had installed the most magnificent *bidet*, plumbed with hot and cold water, the faucets gold-plated. As the youngest daughter I was given the privilege of being the first to use it. I prepared myself and sat down. Believe me, I was thrilled. Then, suddenly, the hot water heater malfunctioned, you know the way they are, the *bidet* gushed scalding water and shattered into a thousand jagged pieces. A terrible experience for an innocent young girl. The thought of it is still so painful that I have never told my friends here about it."

"I'm glad you've finally confessed," Claude said. "It would obviously be very indelicate of us to take up this gentleman's kind offer, in these circumstances."

"You *are* considerate," Aussim said.

The Arab, looking bemused, left.

Lady Sybil liked to hear these stories, and liked Sarah to draw for her full-length sketches of the people involved, but warned us never, under any circumstances, to introduce her to any of them, ending, "I cherish my purity, you know."

One day, at lunch in her apartment, I told her of, and Sarah drew, a man we had been introduced to at Bricktop's who impersonated a Russian Prince. He was so amusing that we took him to my mother's. He succumbed, utterly, to my mother's blandishments and made such a glorious fool of himself that she asked him again. The second time he gave her the second volume of a two-volume edition of Oswald Spengler's *Decline of the West* with a flowery inscription to the "Prince" from, purportedly, the author.

"She couldn't resist him," Lady Sybil said.

"Would you like to meet her?" I asked.

"No. I prefer her as a figment of your perfervid imagination. If I ever meet her I shall cut her dead, and you will have to explain my obnoxious behavior, later."

When I told my mother of that she exploded in delighted laughter. Lady Sybil went on, "But tell me about Aussim's practical tricks, as you call them."

"They're effects, or mimes, rather than buckets of water on top of the slightly open door. The other day we arranged to meet at Maxim's, late. We talked for two hours. Just before we were about to leave Aussim got up, stood in the aisle between the tables, reached under her skirt and slowly pulled out a huge white bath towel. God knows how long she had had it there. Then she carefully folded it up and hung it over her arm, the way a waiter holds his napkin. It was like a dream, very slow, calm, deliberate."

"She's not a lady. I would have thought that Pytor, from what you have told me of him, would prefer ladies to magicians."

"So would I. That's why I find Aussim such an odd choice on his part."

"I think you will find that Aussim is a diversion, and that Pytor is actually in love with Monique. Can he wake the sleeping beauty without damaging both her and her brother, and thus himself?"

"Oh, I would think so. Their relationship is extraordinarily close, but they will grow up, become less dependent on each other."

"What you actually mean is 'seek mates,' isn't it?"

"Yes, if you must put it that way."

"And why don't you, prevaricating little rascal?"

"Because it's too bald a phrase. Part of growing up, for them, is to release each other."

"I don't think that you are necessarily right. It is of course the common notion. The sex urge and all that. But among creative people separating is often not a part of growing up. It is quite possible that Claude and Monique will always enjoy the same relationship they do now. As you know, I am sure, my brother and I have now, and have always had, the same kind of relationship. He is the person closest to me, and I to him. We have no secrets and no messes. Life without him, if it should ever come to that, is inconceivable to me."

I could not imagine asking Lady Sybil about either her sex or her romantic life, and so said nothing, waiting for her to go on, if she chose. She did.

"When I was nineteen an attractive boy fell in love with me. There was a romantic flow between us. I watched him with fascination. He wanted a physical relationship with me. I couldn't understand it. I wanted, then, to be a scholar of poetry. I had my love for him, his for me, and my brother. That was enough. After two years he gave up and married somebody else. I was hurt, and wondered about sex. I asked John Appelby" (a famous older English novelist) "if he would sleep with me. I went to his London flat and spent a week with him. I watched myself and him constantly. Now I am doing this, now he is doing that. My romantic feeling for him was in no way altered, nor my feeling for my brother. Both men, as you know, are extraordinarily talented. Our sense of each other, as creative people, is our bond. Sex was neither agreeable nor disagreeable, it was simply irrelevant.

"So, you see, Monique and Claude may never grow up, as you put it. Their bond may be sufficient. If it is, and if Pytor is in love with her, and equates love and sex as you do, he is bound to be hurt, as I hurt that young man long ago."

It was an end, more depressing to me than usual with Lady Sybil. We said our goodbyes and went to Sarah's. She was to meet Monique there. They were going to a concert by the Budapest String Quartet. I was going to study for an exam the next day, with Claude, at the fountain of the three P's. Monique honked horribly from below. Sarah ran out. I went out onto the balcony to wave and blow Monique a kiss. Sarah emerged and squeezed into the car. Monique banged off as Claude did when he was driving. They were both fiendish. Monique added a peppering of very bad language, which never failed to shock me.

I stayed on the balcony thinking of the agony of my love for Sarah, and then of the three P's. It was time to rename them. The Palpably Phallic Paragons would no longer do. The problem seemed more complicated than it had three and a half years ago, the worship of phalluses an arcane idea, the notion "paragon" distasteful. I imagined the three figures cleaned, in their original pink limestone, and thought that in such guise the male would be reduced, the two females increased, and that the shoe would be on the other foot. Without their soot they might become a Polite Pubic Portent. I determined to work at the problem, some other time.

Aussim came through the gate from the garden, walking fast and looking gloomy. She looked up and waved. I blew her a kiss. She disappeared under the marquee. I opened the door and waited for her. She came in, we shook hands.

"Is Sarah here?"

"No. She's gone to a concert."

"Can I talk to you? I know you have an exam."

"Of course, my dear. It's not that much of a jam. Sit down."

"Why do I always fail with Pytor?"

"What brought this on?"

"I haven't seen or heard from him for two days. I called his house and they say he is not there. But it's not that so much. It's that he's always moody. He withdraws so much of the time. He makes me feel unwanted. I don't expect him to love me, really. It's that he won't let me cheer him up, he won't be *with* me so much of the time."

"You're not necessarily failing, you know. Pytor has tremendous problems. He feels unformed, out of touch with reality. Somehow the things he has learned have not reinforced him yet. I think he has enormous potential, which he feels he is unable to tap. So he's frustrated a lot of the time. He needs inner privacy. In a way he's waiting. He will not become less moody soon. The things he wants are difficult to attain."

I felt that Aussim found all that difficult to understand,

so I went over the ground again, trying to make Pytor's problems more graphic for her. I could feel her, finally, arraying the facts. I asked her, "If he's really too difficult, why not give him up for a more sympathetic type?"

"Not yet. I want to try."

"Concentrate on his outer life."

"Will you get him for me?"

"I'll try. Will you wait here?"

"Yes. It's better here."

I walked directly to Professor Piatagorsky's house. I was sure Pytor was there and had told the servants to say he was out. A cute maid answered the door, whom I knew well, as I had an appointment there for a crit every few days. I asked for Pytor.

"Monsieur Pytor is not at home."

"Then I'll wait for him in his room."

"I'm afraid that's impossible."

I grabbed her, tilted her sideways, gave her a big silent-film kiss, straightened her up and, avoiding the elevator, made for the stairs.

"You're a very very very naughty boy," she called after me.

"I try," I said.

On the way up I met Professor Piatagorsky. We shook hands.

"You don't have an appointment with me, so I assume you are going to see Pytor."

"Yes."

"Good. Get him out of the house."

"I'll try."

I knocked on Pytor's door and walked in. The room was darkened, in a gray haze of acrid smoke. He was lying on the bed, only his trousers on, a cigarette stuck to his lower lip, a large ashtray by his side, filled with butts.

"Ah, it's you," he said.

"Who else, my poor friend."

We shook hands. I sat down on the edge of the bed, asking him, "How goes it?"

"All right."

"But you're suffering."

"Yes. Let's not talk about it. Why are you here? How did you know I was here?"

"Aussim is at Sarah's. I guessed."

"Ah yes. Is she very unhappy?"

"Yes."

"It's beastly."

"No. It's sad."

"I can't behave."

"You can, my dear."

"You can't imagine how I feel."

"Then it's really Monique?"

"Yes. Does it show that much?"

"No."

"Then how did you guess?"

"I didn't."

"Sarah?"

"No."

"I can't understand you. You're talking in riddles."

"Don't worry, the person who guessed doesn't even know you. It was a logical assumption. Have you told Monique?"

"Yes."

He looked in tremendous pain.

"Tell me about it, my dear friend."

"It was in your room. You and Claude and Sarah had gone to classes. Monique and I stayed. You probably remember."

"Yes."

"We danced."

"Yes."

"I kissed her."

"Did she kiss you?"

"Yes."

"Then what?"

"She said, 'Thank you, my pet.' "

"And then?"

"She said, 'You mustn't fall in love with me. It would ruin our relationship, and I value that.' So then I knew. You know her perfume?"

"Get dressed."

He got up. I lay down on the warm bed and lit one of his cigarettes.

"Are you going to wait until Claude grows up and releases Monique?"

"What else can I do?"

"Nothing."

When he was dressed I said, "Aussim is waiting at Sarah's. What shall I tell her?"

"Nothing. I'll go with you."

"This may not take forever, you know. Nothing is permanent."

"I kept thinking that when you guessed it would change our relationship."

"Everything is in flux anyway. I shall mourn for you, dear friend, but then I always have. It's one of my specialties. Nothing can change that."

"Perhaps, now, I can begin to wait."

"That can be learned, I think. But do it actively, this time. Aussim will help you if you let her. She's a professional."

"I know. I'll tell her."

At Sarah's Pytor kissed Aussim warmly. They both looked infinitely sad. He took her arm. They left. Half-heartedly, painfully, I got my books and went to meet Claude at the three P's, over an hour late.

At five I went back to Sarah's longing for her, hoping that she would be back from the concert. Half-past six went by with no Sarah. Then seven. I began to be alarmed. At half-past seven I left a note for her and went to my room. She was not there. I left another note and went to the Post Office to call Monique. When she came on I asked, "Is Sarah with you?"

"No. I left her at the Crillon Bar, about six."

"Why did she stay?"

"A boy she knew came in."

"What was his name?"

"Nelson something. I didn't get his last name."

I was stunned. Bad Clutch!

"Are you there?"

"Yes."

"He was an American. A disagreeable type. He claimed to be a friend of yours. Is he?"

"Yes. We were brought up together. And you're right. He's thoroughly disagreeable. About the most disagreeable person I know, in fact."

"Oh dear. But don't worry, my pet. I'm sure there must be some reasonable explanation."

"I won't, and thanks."

I hung up, feeling sick with apprehension. In her room I paced back and forth, agonized by horrible fantasies of what was happening, at the Crillon, at that very moment. I considered going there and decided not to, again and again, finally went out on the balcony to watch for her. After an interminable wait, every second an agony in itself, a taxi pulled up. Sarah got out. She crossed the sidewalk without paying the driver, disappeared under the marquee. The taxi drove off, so I assumed that Bad Clutch was in it. I turned around, leaning against the wrought-iron railing, and faced the door.

She came in, gave me a short look, went to the bed, and threw herself, face down, on it. I came in. She said nothing. My panic changed to fury. Finally I said, "What happened?"

"I don't want to tell you."

"If you don't, I'll beat you."

I wanted to anyway.

"I was with Bad Clutch."

"Why?"

"I was at the Crillon bar with Monique. He came in. Monique had to go. He asked me if I would like to go up to his mother's suite. I said yes."

"Why?"

"I was curious."

"Was his mother there?"

"For a little. She was going to a cocktail party."

"Then what?"

"He asked me if I wanted a drink."

"So?"

"I said yes."

"Go on."

"I asked for a gin fizz."

"Why, in God's name?"

"I wanted to seem . . ."

"Did you drink it?"

"Some of it. I don't know. Then I forgot the time. He talked on and on the way he does. Then he started to make love to me."

"Did you let him?"

"Yes."

"Then what?"

"He ordered canapés."

"Did you eat them?"

"Yes. Then I began to come to my senses."

"Then what?"

"He started to make love again. I pushed him off and said I had to go. Then he grabbed me, threw me on the sofa, and pulled up my dress. I screamed. He put his hand over my mouth and nose and said he would take me home in a taxi if I stopped. While I straightened out and combed my hair he made a telephone call. We went down and got in one. On the way he stopped it somewhere, I don't know."

"Go on."

"A whore was waiting there. She got in. He sat on the jump seat opposite her and felt her breasts. He said dirty things to her—and to me."

"What dirty things?"

"Like how does it feel to be an architect's whore."

"What else?"

"You could use a merkin."

"Then what?"

"I tried to get out. He yanked me back so hard I fell on the whore's breasts. She screamed. The taxi started to stop.

He yelled furiously at the driver and the whore. Then we were here."

"Good God."

"You'd better go now."

I left, so mad I couldn't believe myself. A sleepless, tortured night followed. In the morning I locked my door and told my waiter when he knocked that I needed nothing. He came back at one and called, "I must see you."

I unlocked the door.

"You and Mademoiselle have had a lovers' quarrel, I understand. She has not taken off her clothes or eaten anything, like you. It's bad for her. She will lose her beauty that way. Go and see her, she needs you."

"I don't feel like it."

"It is a well known fact that lovers have quarrels. Also that they can be made up. It's only the rest of us who quarrel permanently. Go and see her."

"Not now."

"You refuse?"

"Yes. For now. I don't know."

I sat at the window all afternoon, hoping she would come, hoping she wouldn't, deciding to go see her, deciding I wouldn't. Around four the hunchbacked goat woman appeared from below the hotel, then one by one five goats on a long rope. They varied surprisingly in size, the smallest half as big as the largest. Their udders swung voluptuously as they stalked along. The procession circled the tree, then aimed at the rue des Chèvres, the goat woman giving her cry at intervals. As they disappeared into the gloom, my mother appeared out of it, a small, enchanting parasol over her head, a small white bag in the crook of her right elbow, white semilong gloves, Victor at heel, alert and responsible. I was flooded with the idea of getting Sarah a parasol—then remembered.

My mother walked languidly, unhurriedly, apparently without a care in the world. She had a tan Leghorn hat on her back, held by a white strap around her neck. Her brown hair brushed her shoulders. Her dress was a tan and tawny print, the bodice tight with very small lace-edged sleeves, a small tight integral belt, a narrow flowing skirt nearly to the ground, lace-edged. The taxi driver, who was leaning against the bonnet of his cab, straightened up and bowed. She bowed her head gracefully and graciously. Victor wagged his tail ecstatically, momentarily. He gave everyone my mother greeted the same quick, cordial welcome. She aimed at my hotel. In the middle of the square she looked up at my window, saw me, smiled up at me, shifted her parasol, waved, and then made three gestures meaning, unlock the door, open the door, I'm coming up.

When she disappeared I thought of her eyes, so large and dark, with the pupils showing below the iris, in her small heart-shaped face. When she looked up, which she did when thinking, the amount of white was extraordinary. When she looked down there was a sudden large eruption of brown warmth. I wondered why she was coming, unannounced, on this particular day. Could she have heard? I opened the door.

She came in finally, at the same leisurely pace. Victor greeted me. She walked straight to the window seat and reclined on it, her parasol in the open window. Victor jumped up on the ledge and looked out, interestedly, at the square. I sat down on my drafting stool. She said, "Tell me about you and Sarah."

"My waiter?"

"Yes, he called. I took the liberty of telling him that you would reimburse him."

"Thanks."

"Come, love, tell me. Start at the beginning."

I started with the evening at the Maisonette. When I finished, she said, "So you were there that evening. How strange. Did you know that his gums became infected? He had to go to the hospital and then have his front teeth out. His mother told me that while the new ones were being made, he stayed in his room, reading and sober for a whole week. Then he went on a week-long bender. She tracked him down in the flat of a taxi driver friend of his, in terrible shape. She found the whole story amusing. A strange woman. Go on."

I told her the rest of it. When I had finished she got up, saying, "I have an appointment with my chiropodist."

That meant, in Motherese, I have no place to go, but I want to get out of here right now. She took my hand and pulled me to the door saying, "Go and see her right now."

On the landing she stopped, shut my door, and got behind me. As we started down she said, "When a lady falls she should always arrange to fall on a gentleman. I just hope I don't fall going down these stairs."

In the arcade she kept right on going, aimed at the taxi, saying, over her shoulder, "Till later, my love."

I stood and watched her go. Her ass swung smugly. Victor's, too. I set off for Sarah's via the rue du Bouc. It was easier to think going that way, and it seemed appropriate to the moment. What to say once there? I forgive you. I forgive you this time but don't do it again. If you promise not to do it again, I will forgive you. I have treated you cruelly, but it's your fault. Forgive me, I have been a brute.

Let's not quarrel, it's such a waste of time. Let's talk it out. None seemed even remotely possible. I knocked on her door. No answer. I knocked again, still not knowing what I was going to do. She called, "Who is it?"

"Me."

I opened the door and went in. The curtains were drawn, the room was dark. She was standing leaning back against the bed, her posture defensive, the first time I had seen her in such guise. I went to her, took off her dress and slip, picked her up, put her on the bed, turned her over and gave her a tremendous slap on the bottom, which shook satisfactorily, then took off my clothes, lay down beside her, and put my arms around her. She said, "Thank you, my love. I really appreciate that. But it will be a long time before I can forgive myself."

Longer, before I can forgive Bad Clutch, I thought, then, shuddering, remembered that I had completely forgotten my exam.

18

One day, when the leaves of the tree in the square had fallen, we were sitting in the arcade at the *bistro*, reading out loud to each other. Sarah was reading me *Sons and Lovers*. I was reading her *Women in Love*. It was cold. The canvas curtain was up on the outside of the boxwood hedge. The waiter had brought us hot chocolate and a charcoal brazier. Our feet were warm, Sarah had a wonderful tailored tweed suit, with hat to match, a scarf, and gloves. She was in a gloomy mood, her eyelids dark. I alternately watched her and read. Her beauty, her posture, suggested that she was about to take off for worlds unknown, propelled by irresistible inner forces. Intent. Unhappy. Tiny ears, with jade earrings, gloomy in the shade. Small dark eyebrows. Reading eyes. Intent luscious mouth. I was suddenly overcome by my sense of her mood, put my book down, pulled her toward me, and rubbed my nose against hers. Both were cold. She gave me a wide-eyed enchanted look, leaving her gloom, I was sure, for only a short moment. I wanted her.

"Stop thinking about New York," I said.

She forgot her gloom. We rubbed noses, ecstatically. A sound of voices from the *bistro*, which I had not been conscious of, suddenly ceased. We looked in and saw a middle-aged man and woman in the aisle, the Second cop, his arm out, apparently ordering them to stop. They looked like

Americans. The cop twirled around and went out the side door. As he strolled by us, going toward the Station, he said, out of the side of his mouth, "Americans. Help! Help!"

I went in and stopped in front of them. The man bellowed, "George Washington!"

"It's quite far from here," I said. "Unless you have a map, it would be best to take a taxi."

"You speak English," he said, still very loud.

"Yes," very softly.

"We were lost," he said, normally.

"We thought the policeman was going to arrest us," she said.

"No. He just wanted you to wait. He doesn't speak English."

"But George Washington is a Paris street," the man said. "He ought to know how to pronounce *that*."

"It's pronounced Vash-ang-*ton* here. I'll tell the taxi driver for you, if you like."

"He's not there. There's no one in the cab."

"He's at the bar."

"We have so much trouble with these strange French ways," she said.

"You'd think they'd be able to pronounce their own streets," he said.

"Let's just walk around here, dear," she said, pleadingly.

I went back to Sarah.

"What happened?" she asked.

I told her, laughing, took her hand and pulled her up. My desire for her was a total ache. We went to my room, made love passionately, and then went back to the *bistro* with our books. Ten minutes later I was conscious of footsteps stopping in front of us. It was the two Americans again.

"We wanted to talk to you," he said. We said nothing.

"We wondered if you would have a drink with us later. I might have a proposition for you."

I was thrilled. Drugs? White slaves? I looked a question at Sarah. She looked back no.

"We'd be glad to," I said, "but why not here?"

"Oh, we couldn't do that," she said. "It's not that it's really immoral, it's just that we can't get used to the idea of drinking outdoors, in public, and all that, like what you were doing. It's not that we're not broadminded."

I puzzled. We had been reading Lawrence and drinking hot chocolate. Then it occurred to me that when they had first appeared, we had been rubbing noses. They amused me.

"Do you know Harry's Bar?" he asked.

"It's the only place we're really at home," she said. "The food is really good there. We don't like French cooking."

"Would you meet us there at five o'clock?" he asked.

"Yes."

He took out a case and handed me a card. It read:

S. Allen Greene Gifts—Furnishings,
732 Fifth Avenue, New York City,
Telephones Plaza 7598, Plaza 7599.

"We'll see you at five," he said.

They left. Sarah said, "You're out of your tiny cretin's mind again."

"No. Hashish! Beautiful naked Zanzibar concubines. International intrigue. Besides, we've never been to Harry's Bar."

"I'm curious too, but I doubt that this will come out too well. And Lady Sybil may have her worst prejudices confirmed. When do we have to leave?"

"Four-thirty."

As we walked to Harry's Bar I began to think about Mrs. S. Allen Greene's morals, so I said, "I think it would be a good idea if we got married this afternoon."

She gave me a startled look. I said, "Oh, not really," and kissed her. We passed a flower store. I pulled her in and got her an enchanting nosegay, in a white, lace-paper cone. She gave me an overwhelming look, nosegay in her face, head bowed, eyes raised, all whites. When we got to Harry's I asked, "Your name, or mine?"

"Make one up."

"S. Rex Plantagenet."

"It's a deal. But what does the S. stand for?"

"Solipsist, dummy. Everybody knows that. Maybe you could call me Solip, for short?"

"I'd love to, but what does it mean?"

"A person who believes that only the self can be known."

"Shades of Pytor?"

"Concentrate on the royalty part."

"And me?"

"S. Regina Plantagenet. Why be a piker?"

"And what does the S. stand for?"

"You, my true love."

We found the Greenes. I introduced us. He said, "Call me Allen. This is Ellen. What will you have to drink?"

"A *Vichy* for Sarah and a *Dubonnet* for me."

"What are those?"

I explained.

"Will they have them here?"

"I don't know."

The waiter appeared, I ordered ours, he ordered Scotch for them, then said, "You speak very good English. Where did you learn it?"

"New York City."

"You're American! And Sarah?"

"The same."

"We thought you were foreigners," Ellen said. "Fancy that. Isn't it a coincidence?"

"But you do speak French?" he asked.

"Yes."

"Both of you?"

"Yes."

We talked of New York for a while. My dreams of white slavery vanished in a slough of banalities.

"You don't sound like a New Yorker," Allen said to me.

"New York is a melting pot."

"Isn't that the truth," Ellen said. "Of course we don't live there. It's just that Allen has his business there. We live in Scarsdale. It's lovely there."

"What are you doing here?" Allen asked.

"Going to school."

"Why?"

"To get an education."

He looked perplexed but apparently decided not to pursue the matter.

"What were you doing when we thought you were French?" Ellen asked. "Studying? Allen and I used to study together in college."

I wanted to say, rubbing noses, but instead said, "No. Reading D. H. Lawrence."

"Isn't he a dirty writer?" Allen looked wary.

"No."

"You don't look like the sort of people who would read dirty books."

"We are, though."

Sarah looked as if she might laugh. I put my hand under the tablecloth to squeeze her knee. I found her hand, clamped on the nosegay.

Allen said, "You should leave books like that to dirty old men."

I'm already a dirty old man, I thought, and have been for years. And Sarah's a dirty old woman. The thought pleased me. Ellen said, "Allen and I used to read a lot when we were in college, but we don't any more, do we, dear?"

"You outgrow it," he said. "You'll see that you will too."

"You're beautifully dressed, dear," Ellen said to Sarah. They began to talk of clothes. Allen began a description of his business. Finally, there was a pause. Allen seemed to be making up his mind about something. He said to me, "You handle yourself well, Rex. The idea why we asked you is this. Ellen wants to buy a Paris gown. I want to buy some French art for my shop, and I haven't been able to find any. I can't get across what I mean. We both want to go to the *Folies-Bergères*. If you would help us we would be glad to pay the going rate. Just one afternoon and evening. All expenses paid."

I looked the question to Sarah. She looked back yes.

"We'd be glad to," I said. "But I don't think you'll like the *Folies-Bergères*."

"Oh, we have to go, don't we, dear. We couldn't go to Paris and not go to the *Folies-Bergères*. I suppose you two have been often. Is it very riskay?"

"We haven't been."

"How strange. What do you do for amusement?"

I wanted to say fuck, but thought better of it.

"Read. Walk."

I wanted to add, and get picked up by you, but thought better of that too. We arranged to meet at their hotel at two the next day. Sarah and I declined dinner, begging a prior engagement. As we walked to her hotel, Sarah held her nosegay to her nose without surcease, swinging along radiating her pleasure in it, filling me with joy so intense it was painful.

19

The next day we had lunch in the arcade at the *bistro*. Paul came across the square. He had on a black bowler, incongruous on his small, large-faced, cherubic head, a form-fitting black overcoat with a velvet collar, paint-stained overalls, and his usual black patent leather dancing pumps. There was a long thin parcel, wrapped in newspaper, under his arm, and a black smudge on his cheek. He kissed Sarah's hand possessively, shook hands with me, and sat down, saying, "How are you, darlings?" sighing disconsolately.

"We're fine," I said. "But you have a black smudge on your cheek."

"It's that horrid black paint."

He sighed.

"What are you painting?" Sarah asked.

"My room. The landlord has relented." In despair.

Paul had the most beautiful small apartment I had ever seen, in the *entresol* of an apartment house owned and lived in by his father and mother. It was directly over the front door, and had a view of the river through a big, low, round-topped plate-glass window. I envied him that.

"Why black?" Sarah asked.

"I'm going to give black masses." Sigh.

"How will they go?"

"I have in mind a black altar with a beautiful white body stretched out on it . . ."

"Mine?" Sarah asked.

"No, divine Sarah. Mine! Tall black candles," he began to unwrap his bundle, "at head . . . and toe . . . incense . . . the God erect . . . showers of semen, glistening in the flickering light . . . a muted gong . . . silence . . . ecstasy . . ."

He held up, at arm's length, two beautiful tall black tapers. Triumph!

"We would love to come," I said.

"Who else will be there?" Sarah asked.

"You have *not* been invited," he said, "or have you?" looking, a true ham, over his shoulder, directly at a smallish man coming along the sidewalk outside the arcade, in Greek robes and sandals. His hair was long, his feet dirty. He stopped in front of us and, looking over our heads, said, "Art is not dead when it is alive."

He walked on. Paul said, "He scares me to death. What in the world do you suppose brought that on?"

"Sarah's sketchbook, I imagine. He's harmless. And you must admit he's a thinker."

"Oh dear." Paul said. "What are you two reading to each other?"

"Work in Progress."

"Are you cramming for the cocktail party the English Bookstore is giving this afternoon?"

"Yes."

"Tell me what I should think about it. My English simply isn't good enough to let me make sense out of it."

"Neither is ours."

"Come, you're finished with lunch. Let's go for a walk and talk about it."

"We can't. We have dates."

"But you never have dates. What's come over you?"

We told him.

"You're mad children," he said, then in ecstasy, "but you're going to see me in person at the *Folies*, at last! at last!" Then, to Sarah, "Where are you going to take her?"

"I thought Aux Printemps. It's about her speed."

"What about the cocktail party? You can't give up Joyce for an insane bit of slumming?"

"We're going, in between the shopping expeditions and *Folies*."

"I'll see you there, if not before," he said, giving Sarah an intent look. It made me vaguely uneasy. He left, tapers under his arm, apparently in a great hurry. We were late, so we took the taxi to Allen and Ellen's hotel. Expense account. When we got there the taxi driver asked, "Shall I pick you up?"

"No," I said, "but stay now and drive us to where we're going. Mademoiselle and Madame to Aux Printemps. Monsieur and me to the rue Vaugirard. We're going shopping with rich Americans."

"What are you up to?"

"We're conducting a social experiment," Sarah said. "We don't know how it will come out."

"Ah! That again."

"Yes. That again."

"You're incorrigible then."

"Yes."

In the first shop Allen and I went to I realized that my plan for the expedition was entirely and disastrously wrong. Near my school, near the river, there was a row of shops selling popular art. We walked there and found a large collection of watercolors and aquatints of cute dogs and cats, nymphs crouched on rocks, cows in fields, and little boys peeing into pools of water. That last was what Allen wanted.

"People like them in powder rooms," he explained.

Sarah and I had arranged to meet in her room, so that she could dress. I found Sarah sitting on the bed, her elbows on her knees, her face in her hands. I put my arms around her, asking, "What happened?" and immediately realized that she was hilarious, not sad at all.

"We went to Aux Printemps and got her 'A Paris Gown.' Not bad. In fact quite good. But it took an awfully long time. She's fat. When we had finally decided—it was terribly expensive considering—she said, 'I want to get something risqué to wear under it, to remind Allen of our Paris days. Will you help me?' We went to lingerie and I saw Paul lurking in the distance, creeping about. Finally he came up to us, saying, 'Fancy meeting you here.' I introduced him to Ellen. Later she said, 'He is charming, isn't he? We get a lot of those in the shop in New York, believe it or not.' He said, 'I'll help you make your selections.' She wanted black lace brassieres, panties and garter belts. At the panties Paul said, 'Can I show you?' He kept holding them around him. Finally, when she wasn't looking, he pressed a pair at me. He said, 'Buy this for me, darling. I'll pay you back. Give them to me at the cocktail party.' They are over there, in that package." She collapsed on the bed, arms outstretched.

The cocktail party was in a book-lined living room, charming, cluttered, full of character. There were three knots of people, each facing a book-lined wall. The odd-shaped space between the three half circles was sparsely occupied. Nearly everyone had a glass in hand but I could not discover where they came from. We went up to one of the knots. I did not recognize the prisoner inside.

"Who is it?" Sarah asked.

"I don't know."

"Damn it. I wish I had brought my stilts."

"Worm your way in."

"Hold this."

She gave me the small package with the black lace panties. I put it in the side pocket of my jacket. Just then a small gap opened up. She leaned over and peered between two waists. Her bottom swelled out marvelously. I wanted, terribly, to rub it. The prisoner looked to be in a suppressed hysterical agony. The conversation, mostly questions leveled at him, was sycophantic and inane.

We moved to another knot. Lady Sybil was inside, less a prisoner, more a lioness at bay. When she glanced my way I gave her a look of mock horror. She returned a fleeting, marvelously malicious smile. I guessed I was going to pay dearly for that bit of *lèse majesté.*

"Who is it?" Sarah asked.

"Lady Sybil."

"How does she look?"

"As if she would like to dismember everyone, particularly me."

"What did you do?"

"Pretended to be horrified."

"You'll get it in the neck for that, little cretin."

"When we tell her about Allen and Ellen and Paul, all will be forgiven."

As we turned to go to the third knot we met Paul.

"Darling," he said to Sarah, in despair, "you didn't bring the package. My heart is broken."

"But I did."

"Where is it?"

She touched my pocket.

"You *are* angels." Then to me, "I'll take it from you when I leave for the theater." Then to Sarah, "Really, this afternoon was such a bore. I waited for you for hours, wondering whether you had changed your mind and gone somewhere else, terrified that she would not get lingerie to go with the new 'Paris Gown.' But thank you, darling. I would never have had the courage to do it myself. You're my saviour."

"Are you going to wear them in the Black Mass?" I asked.

"Yes."

"How will you get your noble tool out? It's going to be awkward. Or will you start with a strip?"

He looked speculatively at Sarah.

"I know you sew beautifully, darling. Would you help me if I show you where?"

"Yes," she said, no longer able to keep from laughing.

"You *are* my angel," he said, only slightly perturbed.

His father came up and, after handshaking, said, "I think you two are a good influence for Paul. He needs to settle down, you know. He needs an example. I'm afraid his mother and I have not been that."

How utterly awful, I thought, speechless. Sarah smiled dazzlingly at him for reply. I took the package out of my jacket and put it, surreptitiously, in Paul's. We said our goodbyes and went to my hotel for love and food. We had plenty of time, and felt in great need of both.

We got the taxi to take us to Allen and Ellen's hotel, and then to the theater. I sat on the jump seat. On the way I pulled back the glass screen and asked the taxi driver if he would pick us up after the show. He was in one of his difficult moods, a little drunk, and made a great hullabaloo about it, on general principles. Allen asked, "What was that all about?"

"I asked him to pick us up, later."

"In the States it wouldn't take all that talk."

"He's in a lugubrious mood."

"He seems to be a friend of yours."

"Yes. I've known him for years."

"How is that?"

"We're neighbors."

"That's strange."

"Don't be inquisitive, dear," Ellen said.

In the lobby large, slick, illustrated programs were being sold for a huge sum each, the cover a bare-breasted Josephine Baker in marabou. Allen asked, "Would you get us one, and one for you, too?"

"I don't think you'll like them."

"Yes, get him one," Ellen said. "He can show it to the boys back home to prove he's been here."

At our seats, she insisted, like a boss cow, that I go in first, then Allen, then her, and then Sarah. She leaned across Allen to say to me, "Now you can translate the riskay parts to him."

The dialogue was fast as a chattering machine gun, so I was perforce spared that task. Paul fascinated me, yet again, in his role as a smiling automaton. I wondered how the girls got all their black and blue spots, and how many storks had been used up to bedeck them in marabou. The *Folies*, I decided, were Black, and Blue, and Marabou. Intermission, with Allen and Ellen, was a sweaty tedium. When the show was all over I put them in the taxi, refused their money, and told the taxi driver I'd pay him later, at the *bistro*. As they drove off, Sarah said, "A truly noble experiment. And I loved the *Folies*. The colors were marvelously vulgar. Let's go often. I want to study them. But, oh dear, Allen and Ellen were almost incredible. They make me want never to go back. We live in a dream here, you know."

"They're funny, in a sort of horrible way, but they embarrass and worry me too. They make me afraid, for the future. Imagine thinking that little boys peeing in pools is French art."

We walked along, silently, gloomily. Suddenly Sarah got in front of me, walking backwards, put her arms around my neck, looked at me so lovingly that my whole being moved.

"I *loved* being married to you, Solip, my darling," she said.

I picked her up and kissed her, passionately, wanting to permeate her.

When we got to the *bistro* the taxi driver said, "You're my Golden Calf."

"Now what?"

"Your rich American offered me a tip, just a little something to drink with. Two hundred francs."

"What!" I was appalled. It was probably more than the driver made in two days.

"I begged him not to. I shut off the engine, not to save gas you understand, but so that I could hear him better. He was talking so loud that it was impossible to understand him even if I could speak American, which I can't, as you well know. I got down on my knees on the sidewalk, begging him, assuring him that you would pay the fare, and a good tip too. Nothing I could do seemed to have any effect, so, finally, I gave in. Can I buy you a drink?"

Part Four

20

One afternoon, during the course of tea with my mother and Victor, she said, abruptly, "I think you should go to the farm this summer."

I knew it must have been on her mind, and felt wary.

"I don't want to."

"Yes. I think you should. You haven't been there for over a year. After all, your roots are there. It's a good thing to check on one's roots every so often."

"I don't have enough money."

"Of course you do."

"No. Sarah doesn't have enough. I couldn't possibly go without her, and I'm not sure she would even entertain the idea."

"My darling, you love the farm. You haven't been sailing or seen St. Christoph in over a year. You look pasty-faced and overworked. You need exercise and sun."

I knew I was being conned, and wondered whether this was a test of Sarah.

"Have you seen Bad Clutch's mother lately? What have you heard about him?"

"I will make up whatever money you need."

"Oh mother. I love the farm, but this is not the moment for me to go there. I'm happy here."

"Talk to Sarah about it. Yes?"

"Yes. What about Bad Clutch's mother?"

"I am going in two weeks. Send me a cable to say when

and where you will arrive. I'll have George meet you."

I told Sarah about the conversation, at dinner.

"Is it a test of me?" she asked.

"Oh my love."

"You know I can't swim or drive a car or sail a boat. I've never even been in one."

"I'll teach you."

"If you keep on teaching me I'll get to be just like you."

"Perish the thought."

"Why did you say no to your mother?"

"Because I like it here. The only person I want to be with is you. The farm will restrict us."

"Why?"

"It's very New England Episcopalian there."

"I would like to check up on my mother. And I suppose it would be a very good thing to check in with Gordon, Lawrence, and Margaret, to show them what I've been doing. Also I do want to see your farm, the real thing you've told me so much about. I want to go, and yet I'm afraid to. Would we have to land in New York?"

"No. We can take the Cunard Line to Boston. But let's not. Let's stay here."

"Let's think about it."

A few days later she said, "I think we should go."

"I do want to show you the farm."

"I want to see it. And I think I should do those two things in New York. I suppose your mother thinks I might fail, and I suppose I might. But I'm willing to try."

"Don't be silly."

I felt profoundly uncomfortable about it, but it was arranged and we set sail, in a manner of speaking.

On the ship I bribed the purser to give us a table for

two. We went to the *boutique* and bought Sarah a bathing suit, the first clothes I had ever given her. She looked marvelous in it, but swimming lessons were impossible for me. She drew so much attention I couldn't stand it. We gave them up, to read and make love in blissful privacy.

The ship docked, in Boston, early in the morning. George, as promised, met us at the pier, in an old Chevrolet touring car, bulging at the sides, dirty, littered with farm odds and ends, a sick lamb on the back seat. After hugging George and introducing him to Sarah, I said,

"The farm has come to the ship."

"So it would seem," she said, looking at the lamb in real distress.

George said, "She was took just afore I had to leave to get you, so I didn't have no time to drop her off at the vet's. We can drop her on the way home."

"Let me drive, George," I said. "I haven't driven a car in ages."

"All right, Joe," he said, getting into the back seat and putting his elbows on the back of the front seat. "But be careful now. Your lady mother would hate to have anything happen to this valuable vehicle. She bought it secondhand from Methuselah, and he bought it when he was a mere boy, hardly older than you are now."

When he had called me Joe, Sarah had given him a puzzled look.

"Tell her about Joe," I said.

"Well, Sarah, you have a mighty nice name. I always liked it. Well when he was nine, ten, around about there, he come to me one day and he says, 'George,' he says, 'I don't like my name. I want a romantic name like yours.' Imagine that! George romantic. 'What will it be,' I says.

'Joe,' he says. 'All right. Joe it is,' I says. And he's been Joe ever since, at least to me he has. Those highbrows in the kitchen didn't go along. Just couldn't get it in their thick noggins. Too complicated for them, I surmise."

George was off. He didn't stop talking, except to carry the lamb in to the vet's. While he was in there I asked Sarah, "Have you noticed how bright and yellow and harsh the light is here, compared with the soft blue light of Paris?"

"Yes. I've been thinking about it all along. It makes ugly things seem uglier. Is it an omen?"

I kissed her as George came back.

"You'll have to give up them Paris ways around here. Around here kissing is allowed behind the woodshed, nowheres else. Everywheres else is immoral. Your grandmother established that rule afore I was knee high to a grasshopper. I wanted to ask her, 'If you was sitting on a stack of bibles would it be all right?' But I never had the fortitude. She scared me, I don't mind saying, worse than any rattlesnake I ever met. Besides, I knew the answer."

And so on. We turned off the asphalt road onto the long straight dirt road which was the farm's spine, arched by trees, stone walls on either side, the fields beyond dotted with sheep. Our house was one of several off it, all belonging to relatives. It was on the left, just before a white wooden bridge over a tidal river. We turned into the driveway, to an instant hullabaloo of dogs, including St. Christoph and Victor. They ran at the car with mock ferocity.

The first section of the house was late seventeenth century, facing the farm road. It had been added to four times, in a line of articulated blocks, paralleling the river, until it finally joined the barn at the back. The driveway paralleled it, a wide mowed field sloping down to the river on the right, the lawn, with four tall wineglass elms on the house side. As I stopped the car at the front door, a bevy of cousins and their friends spurted from it, all shouting at once. I got out. The big ones kissed me and jumped up and down, the little ones shrieking and the dogs barking, ran around and around the car and jumped on me. St. Christoph put his paws on my chest and licked my face whenever he had the chance. It was typical farm style pandemonium. Departures were also celebrated with the same wild abandon.

My mother appeared, calm and unhurried, waved, kissed me, rebuked Victor, and said to Sarah, "Welcome, my dear."

I went around the car to open the door for her.

"Will the dogs jump on me too?" she asked, looking worried.

"I'll stave them off if they try. Don't pay any attention to them."

My mother said, "Come in and talk to the girls. The boys are off on a cruise. They won't be back until tomorrow sometime."

In the living room, in the oldest part of the house, St. Christoph sat on my lap, until put off in favor of two adorable, cuddly, limp little girls, who liked to be tickled and kissed. St. Christoph, resigned, put his chin on the top of my shoe. Everybody talked at once, tacitly accepting Sarah, fundamentally questioning her. They were nice but assumed too much. As soon as I could I put off the two adorables and said to my mother, "I want to show Sarah the farm, before lunch. We'll have to change. Where have you put us?"

"Sarah in the pink room, on the second floor. You in the blue room, near the barn."

I groaned, inwardly, agonized by the idea of being separated from her at night. I thought of the mill, and of how marvelous it would be to make love in that supremely romantic, aromatic, great loft of a space, to the sound of water cascading over the dam. But we would still wake up in separate beds, on separate floors, far apart.

I took her to her room, St. Christoph preceding us, his toenails clicking on the spattered pine corridor floors, long, whitewalled, narrow in places, wide in others, around corners, by window embrasures, upstairs, down a step, to the Pink Room, where I kissed her, lovingly.

She said, "We're not to have adjoining rooms, then?"

"No. I had hoped for that, but I suppose my mother wants to avoid any possibility of gossip. We can make love, though. There are hundreds of places. The main thing is that I want to wake up with you, to see you and feel you first thing. I don't know how I'm going to do without that. Anyway, get into some washable things."

Sarah liked the farm buildings, but was afraid of the animals. Lunch, a picnic on the lawn, with a lot of miscellaneous children, one of the adorable little girls in my lap, was chaotic. After it I said to Sarah, "Come. Let's go sailing. I want to take you before you go to New York tomorrow. Put on a bathing suit, it may be wet, and bring a warm sweater, it might get chilly."

We put on our bathing suits separately, met on the lawn, and walked single file, Sarah first, along a narrow path through woods, which led to the landing. St. Christoph charged back and forth in ecstasy, brushing us as he went by, until I saw that he really distressed Sarah, making her flinch each time, and told him to heel. George had put my boat in the water and rigged it. It was a small centerboard sloop, twelve feet on the water with a four-foot plank bowsprit, gaff-rigged, drawing about a foot with centerboard up, about a foot of freeboard, no sheer, no ballast, wide mahogany decks to sit on, a narrow cockpit for feet, from forward of the tiller post to forward of the centerboard trunk. A Victorian dream of a skimming dish, very comfortable, if a little wet. There were few left from the time it had been a popular racing class. I cherished her, had renamed her every year until I came to *Aglaia*, where I stopped, because people laughed at me every spring. I showed Sarah how to bend the sails, warned her to duck her head every time I said "Ready about," and we shoved off, St. Christoph in his usual spot, front feet on the bowsprit, hind feet on deck, peering into the water, looking for horseshoe crabs. He dove for them, also occasionally fell overboard, his head thump-thumping along the bottom of the boat before he appeared in the swirl of the wake.

Wind and tide were coming in, the water smooth and opaque. It took several short quick tacks to get to the river's mouth. I felt exhilarated. When we reached the sea, tide and current fought, causing a short chop. The bowsprit pushed up water and threw back showers of glistening droplets, causing St. Christoph to duck, comically. I laughed. No longer needing to tack, I fastened the jib sheet, held the main sheet and tiller in one hand, and put my other arm around Sarah's waist. It was warm, the sun was warm, the sea beyond the chop glimmered smoothly. It should have been bliss, but Sarah was tense and withdrawn. I kissed her.

"Are you scared?"

"Yes. I can't help it. It tips so."

"Heels. It's supposed to."

"What if it should just dig in in front and go down. I can't swim."

"It's as old as the hills and hasn't done it yet. It can't sink, you know. It floats when it's full of water. I've had it full several times. There is a club, world renowned, consisting of all the former owners of *Aglaia*. The oldest member is a hundred. I am, obviously, the youngest. And if you will put your arm around me, and hug me with all your might, you'll be able to tell that I'm still alive too. Come, my love, relax. It's marvelous fun."

"I can't."

I gave her the mainsheet, saying, "Hold that. If you get scared, let go."

The next time a puff came along, I said, "Let go."

The boat rocked back level, the mainsail flapping loudly. Sarah gasped, obviously terrified, then said, "It's fiendish."

"Oh my darling, it's only a gadget."

I freed the sheets, took off her bathing suit and mine, pressed her down into the cockpit, got on top of her, and kissed her. She was tremendously receptive and still scared. We coupled. In full flight *Aglaia* knocked over, violently, dousing us with a great wallop of water and tumbling us against the side of the cockpit. I jumped aft, on top of Sarah, shook out the tangle of the mainsheet, and slammed the tiller over. The feet of both sails were in the water, she righted gently, and I saw that all our clothes, and St. Christoph, had been thrown into the drink. He swam around to the stern, his fur wet, his beast's eyes uncovered, gleaming with excitement. I hauled him on board by the scruff of his neck. He shook himself, showering us, and hippety-hopped around the deck, utterly delighted. Sarah sat up, put her head in her arms on the deck, and trembled. She looked incredibly beautiful, profoundly shocked.

"Sarah darling, it wasn't dangerous. It's all right. Forgive me."

I sat down in the cockpit and put my arms around her.

"Take me home."

I got the boat going, running free, wing and wing, toward the beach, on our side of the river's mouth, hauling up the centerboard on the way.

"Where's my bathing suit?"

"Lost. We lost all our clothes."

"But I can't go to your mother's without clothes on."

"Sarah darling. We'll cope."

At the beach I let go the halyards and ran *Aglaia* up on the sand. Sarah shuddered. I got out the anchor, ran with it till the rope was taut, and ran back to Sarah.

"My knees are wobbly."

I picked her up, took her to a hot sand pocket, put her down, lay down beside her and held her tightly. St. Christoph ran around and around us, at top speed, exuberantly, kicking up sand, until I yelled at him to lie down. When Sarah stopped shivering I took off the sails and wrapped her in the jib, myself in the mainsail, Roman fashion. She helped, and looked marvelous, one shoulder bare, the snaps on the luff diagonally across her body, marvelously ornamental, one sheet wrapped around her waist, twice, and looped. We started along the path to our house. On the way we met two adorable little boys. One said, "What are you two sillies doing in those sails?"

The other, banging St. Christoph on the head with his fists, to keep from being slobbered, said, "They're wet. I bet they campsized."

The first said, "Yeh, in their birthday suits."

"We're playing Romans," I said, "going to the Forum to see the Lions eat the Early Christian Children."

They seemed impressed. We squeezed by them and went on, Sarah still in a state of mild shock. I steered her to her room, went to mine, put on another bathing suit, spread the mainsail out on the back lawn, went to her room, shut and locked the door, opened the screen, and threw the jib out the window. St. Christoph followed each move with great interest. Sarah was on the bed with a quilt over her. I sat down on the edge, took her hand, and said every silly thing one can say in such circumstances. She said very little. After about an hour she began to recover.

"I can't do that," she said. "It's worse than anything."

"Sarah, please, you don't have to do it. It was inexcusable of me to let that happen on your first time out. I should have taught you to swim first, and then to doodle about in the river. Or at least put you in a life jacket."

"Like a good daddy."

"Oh Sarah!"

I lay down on her, in anguish. Why had I frightened her at the very moment I had wanted to reassure her? St. Christoph thumped his tail on the floor.

2 1

The next morning I woke her at six. We had a hurried breakfast in the kitchen. I got my mother's Mercedes to take her to the train, leaving St. Christoph behind. When we turned out of the farm road onto the asphalt, I took her hand and said, "Sarah."

"Yes."

"I love you, you know, more than anything else in the whole wide world. Ever since I first met you, that night at my mother's, you have pervaded every moment of my life. My whole being is continuously involved with you. I adore you as you are gay, and sad, and gloomy, and perceptive about things. With you I feel informed, formed, completed. I adore your way of being talented, unexpected, silent, warm, childish, afraid, feminine. Sometimes I love your ears so much I'm afraid my heart will break. Other times it's something you say, and the way you say it. Remember that, all the time you're in New York."

"Yes."

We were silent the rest of the way to the South Station, holding hands tightly. There she said, "Meet me at seven o'clock in the morning the day after tomorrow," and hurried aboard the train. I followed with her bag and drawings. She gave me a peck. I felt she wanted to be alone, so I left, waiting, out of her sight, until the train pulled away, chugging, straining, steaming.

"Who will take care of her?"

The next thing I was conscious of was the rumble of the wood planks of the ramp up into the barn, under the Mercedes' front wheels. I was going too fast. Suddenly horrified, I realized that I could not remember any conscious decisions since the train had left, not even having put down the canvas top. I parked the car in the box stall and imagined what was going on in the house, the maid downstairs, bustling about with brooms, carpet sweepers, and dusters, plumping pillows, the cook bustling around the kitchen, with breakfast and breakfast dishes, upstairs my mother ensconced in her bed, where she would spend the morning having breakfast, reading, writing letters, telephoning, planning, and entertaining family and servants. I was often summoned, and enjoyed those constantly interrupted sessions, but today wanted no part of that scene. St. Christoph came in. I went to the back of the barn, took the ladder down into the lower level, even with the ground there, walked down to the river, out of sight of the house, and then along the river path to the landing, got *Aglaia* going and, beyond the chop at the river's mouth, took off my clothes, put them in the sail bag, put that in the forepeak, then came to, in agony.

"Who will take care of Sarah?"

I took a broad reach, south, out into the Atlantic, adumbrating madly.

When I got back to the landing, late that afternoon, I took the same path I had come by back to the barn, took my mother's Mercedes to the village drugstore, bought two packages of cigarettes and some matches. I had heard that they decreased sexual longing, and supposed that was why Pytor had smoked so much that day. The first one, anyway, didn't help. I smoked it while telephoning at the back of the drugstore. When I finally got Sarah's mother's number, a woman's voice answered, a voice that I was sure was not her mother's. I asked for Sarah. There was a long pause. The voice asked for my name. I told her. Another long pause. Then the voice said, "Hello."

"Yes."

"I'm sorry, but she can't talk to you now."

The line went click, dead.

The next thirty-six hours were the most miserable of my life to that date. At four-thirty in the morning of the second day I could stand it no longer, got dressed, went to the barn, took a black Ford sedan used by the servants, and left for the South Station, leaving St. Christoph behind. In the depressing, smelly, marble lunchroom I got coffee and doughnuts and went to a table. Sarah came in almost immediately, an hour early, without baggage. Her face told me instantly that she was in great pain. It was swollen and contorted, as it had been a year earlier, while she told me of her life. She sat down opposite me and said, in a rush, "I accepted a full partnership with Lawrence Palladine, starting now. I wasn't going to come back, and then I couldn't stand not seeing you one last time. I sat in Grand Central for an hour trying to decide, and then I was on the train. I wanted to see you knowing I would never see you again. I wanted you to see me knowing you would never see me again. Do you think that's selfish? I want you to hate me."

"Sarah! Sarah! Don't. Let me get you some coffee."

I got up.

"No, I feel sick."

I pushed her into the inner chair, sat down beside her, and put my arm around her. She said, "Don't seduce me.

My mind is made up. You'll just make it worse."

"Sarah. What's come over you? You seduce me all the time. That's what love's all about."

"No. It isn't. You don't understand. I want you more than anything else in the world, and I've had you for a year, but I can't really have you, you know that, and as I can't then at least I can have a career of my own, and I have to settle for that. I mean it's a necessity."

"But you do have me—more than ever. I meant what I told you driving to the station. Why did you take this partnership?"

"Because it's a chance in a lifetime. It would be stupid to turn it down, in spite of school. I can take courses in New York."

"Then why can't we live together in New York. I can go to Columbia Architectural School, it's supposed to be improving."

"No. We can't. If we were to try that you couldn't love me any more and I would end up a real mess."

"Why, Sarah darling?"

"For one thing you have to lead your orderly existence and want to see people you like. Claude, Pytor, Monique. And Lady Sybil. I will have to see other people, and would, will, be in a frantic turmoil most of the time. We would never be able to do anything together, you'd always have one thing and me another. The people we would want to see won't like or understand each other. We wouldn't be able to commune, which is the real basis of our love."

"But why can't we work out some *modus vivendi*, just as we did in Paris."

"You don't know me in my world. I have been in yours, and know how different it is from mine, and how difficult it is for me. You couldn't think of poking my sister because your fastidiousness would get in the way. I sealed my contract with Lawrence Palladine on my knees, with his cock in my mouth, sucking."

"Oh Sarah! Please! I don't believe it. Stop it. Come to your senses. I love you. You must know that."

"It's the truth. I told you I want you to hate me. You are never trapped by people, not even Lady Sybil. I'm easily trapped by them, like Bad Clutch. When I'm nervous I want to make an impression, and do something silly and cheap. You don't know that about me, except that once, and that made you madder than you've ever been. You protected me from that in Paris. You made a life for me. In New York you won't be able to. I know I can't have you, and as I can't I have to have a career, and that has to be on its own terms and conditions. You'd hate those, and then hate me.

"You have a lot of school left. I am going to make money immediately. It will be years before you do. You are looking towards enduring things while I'm looking towards ephemera. You don't realize how protected you are by your family and your early training. I am not. All I have is talent and dedication. But that's enough. You weren't nicknamed Alarm Clock for nothing. You put your school life together as if you were making a clock, and you are unusually capable of causing and feeling alarm. It scares me, knowing myself. I simply can't work the way you do. I'll never, really, be able to do it. It's like ballet, or sailboats. You have to start young. I didn't. You'd get tired of watching me when you could no longer teach me. Poor work habits are unaesthetic in your eyes.

"Think of Monique. She has everything you like except

raw talent, but you have enough of that to fill your need. Can you imagine what it would do to us if our sense of dedication clashed, or if we should attack each other's sense of talent? From now on we can only destroy each other."

"Oh Sarah, I love you."

"I know myself. You don't. You can't really love me because you don't really know me. You're in love with a dream of me. You can't imagine what it's like to be beautiful. I cheated you—remember. The reason I could was because you thought of me as a nymph. If I hadn't been beautiful you would never have loved me. As it turned out, I could help you, but that doesn't change the basic thing which is that I can't really have you. Can you imagine marrying me? No real background, no babies, no real understanding of what makes your mother and her friends tick, no feeling for dogs, animals, cooking, boats, children. You love all those things and will have to have them. I know that. I can feel it."

I put my elbows on the table, my face in my palms. There was a long agonized silence. She went on, "I can live in a messy New York apartment and go to lunch in the country every fifth Sunday, and live with it. You couldn't. Our love in Paris was in a vacuum, supported by the city and our isolation. Now, after the farm, I have the missing clue to you. You don't have the missing clue to me."

"Please, Sarah. Then let me see it, or at least try it and find out for myself."

"No. I've seen both worlds, and I'm far too terrified to let this go on. I'm not going to see you, ever again. I said just now that I wanted you to hate me. I don't. I want you to love me always, somewhere inside you because I shall always love you."

After a long pause she said, despairingly, "Will you walk me to the train now?"

We got up. She took my arm. At the train she said, "I hate myself for being out of your reach, and I hate you for being out of mine."

The conductor helped her up the steep steps to the platform. She gave me a long last heartbreaking look.

"It was a dream," she said, and disappeared, shattering my life.